Viral Learning

Also by Mary Griffith

The Homeschooling Handbook
From Preschool to High School, A Parent's Guide

The Unschooling Handbook
How to Use the Whole World As Your Child's Classroom

Viral Learning

REFLECTIONS ON THE HOMESCHOOLING LIFE

Mary Griffith

ISBN 978-1-4303-1217-8

Portions of the Introduction were originally published in slightly different form in "Confessions of a Famous Homeschool Author," in Tammy Cardwell, ed., *See, I Told Me So!* Baytown, Texas: CJ Press, 2005. 59–61.

Published by LULU

Printed in the United States of America

Table of Contents

Acknowledgments

Writing this book has been a much different experience from my earlier books, since I decided right from the beginning to publish it with a print-on-demand (POD) company instead of looking for a traditional publisher. As pleasant as my editors were to work with—at least compared with the experiences that other writers I know had with other editors—I loved the idea of being in charge of every detail of my book.

It wasn't just control over the content. My editors were usually pretty easy to persuade when I felt strongly about what I wanted to write. But I was tickled at the idea of holding complete power over the look and feel of the layout and design, and of not having to cringe at the wording of the cover copy or marketing materials, even if I would have to write them myself.

Foolish it may be, to be one's own editor, but at least it's not as dangerous as serving as one's own doctor or lawyer. The risk is simply that of making myself look foolish (and I've had practice at that). I am, to a greater extent than most authors, utterly and comprehensively responsible for every word, every letter, every punctuation mark, and every blank space contained herein.

Having said that, there are—of course!—more than a few people without whose help I would never have finished the book.

First and foremost among those are everyone who responded to my request for answers to an entirely too long list of open-ended questions about their lives and their thoughts about homeschooling and learning in general. Even though I didn't use everything everybody had to tell me, what they had to say was tremendously helpful in making me think hard about what I had to say myself.

Shannon Anderson, Maureen Berger, Julia Biales, Myranda Brown, Leslie Buchanan, Donald Burris II, Mary Gold, Leslie McColgin, and Christine Sanders were new contributors with this book, though several of them I've known for years through online forums and mailing lists and in-person homeschool groups. I'm especially grateful to Joyce Fetteroll, Samantha Fenner, Sandra Dodd, and Jo Craddock, who also participated with *The Unschooling Handbook* and came back, anyway. And I am extraordinarily indebted to Carol Burris, Tammy Cardwell, and the indefatigable Lillian Jones, who've written pages and pages for me for three books now.

I also need to thank a few people for general moral support over the past couple of decades: The gang from the Northern California Homeschool Association that was and the HomeSchool Association of California as it is now, especially Melissa Hatheway, Barbara Falcon, and minor toy magnate Kim Stuffelbeam, who first taught me about designing for print but bears no blame for my design shortcomings. Helen and Mark Hegener, of *Home Education Magazine*, have always been generously supportive (even when we've differed on some of the politics of homeschooling).

And for general inspiration, I owe huge thanks to Micki and David Colfax, whose *Hard Times in Paradise* can still make me laugh. Nobody ever has better stories at conferences than they do, and more importantly, they've always demonstrated that even when we're in the midst of it, homeschooling isn't the most important thing in the world.

Finally, I'm indebted to the pair who taught me more about learning than everybody else put together—as I said in the first edition of *The Homeschooling Handbook,* "to Christie and Kate, who are the whole point."

Viral Learning

Introduction

The introduction to the 1997 first edition of my first book, *The Homeschooling Handbook,* started out with this little hypothetical chat:

> Announcement: "We're homeschooling our kids."
>
> Response ten years ago: "You're doing what? What's that?"
>
> Response today: "Oh, yeah? I know someone who does that. But I could never do it myself — it would be so much work!"

I went on to talk about how homeschooling had grown from a relatively rare and eccentric practice to become one of the fastest-growing educational movements in the country.

Today, after another decade, the homeschooling movement is still growing and changing, but along with the

---

* Part of this material was published in different form in the essay, "Confessions of a Famous Homeschool Author," in Tammy Cardwell's collection, *See, I Told Me So!* (Baytown, Texas: CJ Press, 2005).

movement, we homeschoolers—the parents and kids and grandparents and assorted family friends who comprise that movement—have also grown and changed as individuals. The process of homeschooling, of thinking about how learning happens and figuring out how best to let it happen within our own families, has affected the ways we think, the ways we approach problems, the ways we live our lives.

That's what this book is about. After both *The Unschooling Handbook* and the revised edition of *The Homeschooling Handbook* were published, my editor asked me what else I wanted to write about homeschooling. What else? What else was there I could write about it? I could imagine books that could be written, about homeschoolers going to college or about homeschooling with special needs kids, but those were topics I hadn't the expertise or interest to write. Perhaps I could work on a series of books for homeschooling different age groups, my editor suggested. No, I thought, with my older daughter barely into her teens, I didn't have enough experience with different age groups to be able to say anything intelligent that I hadn't already said in my existing books. And I didn't want to write a book with nothing new in it—recombining and rehashing the same old stuff in pretty new packaging would have felt too much like fraud.

It's not as though I'd deliberately set out to become a Famous Homeschool Author. It was very nearly an accident that I wrote my books at all. A year or so after we'd begun homeschooling, I'd started to work with a state homeschool support group. (I'd sent a letter to the newsletter editor offering to help, and the reply was essentially, "How would you like to be the new editor?") Several of us on the group's board fantasized from time to time about one day writing a book about homeschooling, but none of us did much of anything to pursue the idea.

Then one day, I got a call from an editor with a company that was considering getting into publishing curriculum for homeschoolers. She wanted to learn about the homeschooling market, so I sent her a big packet of information, including our newsletter, other homeschooling publications, and a list of other resources, and thought no more about it. But a couple of weeks later, she asked me up to the publisher's offices where I was introduced to a small flock of editors around a very large conference table. These editors asked lots of questions about homeschooling. They said they planned to put together a test package, and asked me to return and give them some feedback when they had something more concrete.

So after another few weeks, I visited the publisher's offices again, and in a smaller conference room, was shown their first attempt at an English curriculum package for homeschoolers.

It was a flat white corrugated cardboard box. ("We'll have some nice colorful graphics on the outside, of course.") Inside the box were a folding game board (blank) and a smaller box that contained cardboard geometric shapes in various colors. ("These will be a board game using a different shape and color for each part of speech.") There was also a good-sized paperbound volume, which I picked up to look through, only to discover that the inside was as blank as its cover. ("We'll hire outside writers to develop the actual content.")

"We're looking," said the editor, "at a price point of $50. Do you think homeschoolers will buy this?"

"No," I said.

They were taken aback that I seemed so certain. I explained again the legendary cheapness of homeschoolers (though that's a tricky thing to get most non-homeschoolers to understand: we are exceedingly cheap, but we'll also spend ridiculous amounts on things we think worthwhile). It was remotely possible, I went on, that homeschoolers might spend that much on a single academic subject, but it would have to be something spectacular, and it would certainly have to have its content available for viewing before any homeschooler would decide that it was spectacular enough to be worth $50.

And that was that, I thought.

But another couple of weeks later, I got a call from a different editor at the same publisher. She told me they'd decided there really wasn't a viable market for them in curriculum, but they thought there might well be a market for a trade book about homeschooling. Would I be interested in writing a proposal for such a book?

Since I'd been lazily thinking about such a project for a couple of years, it didn't take me long to come up with an outline, a market analysis, and the other bits and pieces for a proposal. About a week after I sent it off, the editor called to accept my proposal for *The Homeschooling Handbook,* in which I would try to provide new homeschoolers with all the information I would have liked to have had when I first started homeschooling.

When *The Homeschooling Handbook* was first published, my daughters were only 13 and 9. We'd been homeschooling all their lives, but we knew lots of families who'd been homeschooling far longer, who'd actually got their kids through high school and into college, and on to adult lives. I thought of myself as someone who'd learned quite a bit from homeschooling, and was lucky enough because of my work with the state support group to have begun to get an idea of the kinds of things other homeschooling families were up to. We were just another homeschooling family trying to figure out what we were doing—except that Mom was suddenly a Famous Homeschool Author.

In 1997, mainstream publishers were only just beginning to discover the potential homeschooling market. John Holt's *Teach Your Own* was available, Warner Books had picked up Micki and David Colfax's originally self-published *Homeschooling for Excellence,* and David Guterson's *Family Matters* had actually been released in hardcover, practically a first for a homeschooling title. Just about everything else in print was either self-published or from a religious publishing house.

Neither I nor my family was prepared for the response *The Homeschooling Handbook* received. I'd spoken at homeschool conferences before, and at not-back-to-school information nights, but always before I'd been just another homeschooling parent, like those in my audience, but with—maybe—a bit more experience. But now that my book was in print, and people could order it from Amazon or walk into a local bookstore and pick a copy off the shelf, many in my audiences apparently believed that what I had to say was more credible and more important than it had been the previous month, before I had become a published author.

Suddenly parents asked questions I didn't know how to answer: How many and which types of arithmetic problems should their six-year-old be doing each day? What time should their nine-year-old be going to bed? If they required their kids to keep journals, what should they make sure their kids wrote about? How could they keep their kids from watching TV or ingesting sugar products when they were at other people's houses?

My daughters thought all these questions were hilarious. Kate, the then-13-year-old, was the one who had come up with the "Famous Homeschool Author" label for my speaking persona, and she managed to invest that title with all the ironic, pitying contempt that a 13-year-old can muster for a deeply uncool parent so obviously lacking the skills and expertise expected of any grown-up, let alone someone who was supposed to know what she was talking about. Christie, nearly four years younger, was more direct: "Mom, why do they ask you things you don't know?"

It's not like I ever pretended to know all the answers to those sorts of questions. My usual reply was to give examples from my own family's experience and from that of other homeschooling families I knew, and to explain that the whole process of homeschooling is a matter of trial and error, of learning what works best with you and your kids this year, and learning how to adapt when your own and their needs and interests change. I always thought this an eminently reasonable response, but more often than you'd think, the questioner would become angry and accuse me of keeping secret some magic that would make the whole process of homeschooling easy, even automatic.

Once *The Homeschooling Handbook* proved itself to be a steady seller, my editors approved my proposal for *The*

Unschooling Handbook, despite their apparent nervousness about it. When that book, too, proved successful, I was set to work on the revision of *The Homeschooling Handbook.* By the time it was published, I had been working on homeschooling books for nearly four years. I was thoroughly sick of writing and reading and thinking about homeschooling. The prospect of producing a new manuscript and all the rereading and tweaking and rereading and editing and rereading and proofing required to get it into print was not one that filled me with enchantment. All I wanted was to get away from that upper-case Homeschooling and retreat back to the ordinary, lower-case variety, to spending time with my girls, exploring a few of the countless interesting things we could find in our normal, quiet, everyday routines.

So I did not write another homeschooling book. By that time, my publishers had recruited a whole stable of homeschooling writers and other publishers had jumped into the market, so there were plenty of homeschooling books being published. With relief, I gave up my Famous Homeschool Author persona (aside from an occasional conference gig every couple of years). Bit by bit, I pulled back from involvement with state and local support groups and turned my duties over to the next wave of homeschooling parents becoming activists.

I did not write another homeschooling book—then.

Inevitably, though, the girls grew up, and as my younger daughter started to look into colleges, I began to wonder about what I would do with life after homeschooling. Would I look for a full-time job? A part-time job different from the one I already had? Should I write more, finally getting around to all those murder mysteries I've been constructing in my mind all these years?

Gradually, I realized that I was thinking more and more about homeschooling again. Now that active homeschooling was coming to an end for our family, I found myself pondering its long-term effects: How different am I from the person I would have been if I'd not been a homeschooling parent? How have my interests and values changed because of our kids learning at home? How are my kids different from their peers? Were we really as eccentric as we thought were? Would we have been eccentric in any case?

What about the homeschooling movement today? Are new homeschoolers really all that different from what I was like when first starting out, less independent and looking for more direction? Are there actually more of those dogmatic "do it my way or you're not a real homeschooler" homeschoolers out there? Or am I just getting cranky? And what about those few "graduated" homeschooling parents (mostly moms, naturally) who seem lost and unwilling to let go of their homeschooling connections once their kids leave home? Are they simply in the midst of the same transition I am, or have they been so wrapped up in their kids' lives they really don't have lives of their own?

At the same time, everything I'd been reading—books, articles, blogs—seemed to connect to what I was thinking about learning and community, even though it wasn't directly related to education or homeschooling. Even when I thought I wasn't thinking about homeschooling, I was thinking about homeschooling. Suddenly, after all these years, I realized there was another homeschooling book in my head.

This book is different from the others, though. I sent out one of my daunting long questionnaires and collected opinions and experiences from homeschoolers across the country, just as I did with the earlier books. But this book isn't another guide to how to homeschool, nor is it meant to help homeschooling parents survive the empty-nest syndrome.

This book is personal. It's a reflection on how I (along with a few of my friends) came to homeschooling, how it affected us and our view of the world, and how those changes in us may spark changes around us.

Of course, to figure out how we ended up here—and just where, exactly, "here" is, we need to start with a look back at how we began our homeschooling adventures.

Learning From My Education

Ten or fifteen years ago, a friend my mother's age who had asked to read a few issues of the homeschooling newsletter I was then editing remarked that "all these people seem to be making decisions based on what happened to them as kids." She thought this was strange, that it was a sign of some sort of widespread neurosis among homeschooling parents, but I always thought it was a fact so obvious as to be almost a tautology: Of course we are products of our past. And of course we make decisions for our children based on our own experience. How could we not?

My own education certainly primed me to become a homeschooling parent. By most conventional measures, I was the epitome of a successful school student: grade point average within a few hundredths of a 4.00 (in those long-ago years before AP and honors courses made 4.00+ GPAs ubiquitous), National Merit finalist, 99th percentile SAT scores, academic scholarship for college—everything to cheer a proud school official's heart and demonstrate the virtues of the local public school system.

I learned a great deal from my schooling. But what I learned was not much what was intended to be taught. There were the obvious disadvantages to school learning that most of us notice early in our school careers—the parceling of knowledge into discrete little packets of "age-appropriate" material beyond which we could not go until next year or junior high or some time other than now, the social effects of spending so much time with so many age-peers and so few adults, the cultivation of obedience and conformity.

But there were other more subtle lessons about learning and what learning was and was not, about what society values in individuals and what we value in ourselves.

Much of what I learned in school took years to unlearn.

Imagine the six-year-old me — very shy, but excited and eager to be in school. Now you have to remember that in the late '50s and early '60s, civilization had not yet advanced to its current state. Kindergartners still just learned colors and took naps and played with blocks and crayons and climbed jungle gyms. The exciting thing about first grade was that we got to start actually learning important things like letters and numbers. One Friday, after a couple of months of learning to form our letters properly with those fat green pencils on lined splintery newsprint, Mrs. Olsen told us that the next Monday would be the day—on Monday we would learn to read and write.

I endured the weekend impatiently. I couldn't wait to ascertain the secret that would open the door to so many of the mysteries of the world of grown-ups.

Monday finally came, and I was poised for the big revelation.

Mrs. Olsen went to the chalkboard, all of us ready with our splintery paper and chunky pencils, and said that if we were careful to get every step right, we would learn to read and write.

The first step was to draw a vertical line. Then we were to connect a shorter horizontal line to it at the bottom. Next came two circles, adding little arcs at the bottom of each, and filling in the spaces we'd created. Then came another vertical line, with two more shorter lines angling out from its center.

"There!" said Mrs. Olsen proudly. "You've written your first word: You can now read and write."

Yes, indeed, there it was: an uppercase "LOOK" with little eyes colored into the bottoms of the Os, a cute-but-dumb visual pun with which to start our real academic careers. Definitely a word. And I had certainly followed all the instructions I'd been given to create my very own copy. But how did that amount to reading and writing? I was outraged. All I'd done was draw some lines exactly as I'd been told, and she was telling me that because of that, I could read? Who was she trying to kid? I couldn't believe the swindle. I didn't understand any more than I had before I'd drawn those line segments so carefully. Where was that big epiphany I'd been waiting for?

Real reading, of course, took months longer, and was the gradual process it is for everybody.

In fourth grade, we had a student teacher. She was young and enthusiastic, and everybody wanted to sit next to her in reading group or help her with the many bulletin board displays she created. One of those displays, up for the last few weeks of the school year, was a "growing" flower garden. She made construction paper daisies, one unique, secret color combination for each of us in the class, crowded together across the bottom of the bulletin board. The stems of the flowers were made of green yarn, and were extended two inches for each test, each quiz, each homework assignment we completed with a perfect 100% score.

Every few days, she'd update the flowers. Many grew a respectable two to four inches each week. Those of us who were good spellers who aced the pre-tests and the vocabulary quizzes and the final spelling tests each week and who had no trouble with the frequent arithmetic quizzes, had flowers that shot up a foot or more each week. And then there was that sprinkling of flowers sitting there at the bottom, stuck at the beginning, unmoving for the entire life of the paper garden.

As she added stem lengths and moved the flowers, the student teacher encouraged us to speculate on who each flower represented. Interestingly, a few students who never got grades beyond average were convinced that some of the tallest blooms were theirs. Several debates over whose flowers were whose grew quite heated, even among those who had no more than one or two perfect grades that month. Somehow, the fact that there was a relationship between actual grades and the heights of each flower got lost.

Eventually, revelation day came. The student teacher called out each color combination and announced the name of the student it belonged to. starting with the still-stunted row at the bottom. Each student then got to walk up to the bulletin board to claim the flower. Many were surprised at how high—or how low—their flowers were. I wasn't. Mine was the flower that had grown beyond the top of the bulletin board, up the wall and onto the acoustic tiles of the ceiling. That was about the time I started believing that my grades meant that I was smarter than the others in my class, which made me a better person than everybody else in my class. Naturally, that meant that maintaining my grades became very important—after all, if my self-worth was defined by being "smart" and being smart depended on my grade point average, every A was crucial.

That was also when I started not much liking the person I was in school.

Let's move on to fifth grade. This incident came courtesy of my mother, who had the peculiar idea that she should tell us what our teachers said about us at parent-teacher conferences. I, the oldest child in my family, was by then a typical overachiever, one of those obnoxious kids who raised her hand for everything and got straight As and completely ruined the curve for everybody else. My brother, a year and a half younger, was smarter but lazier--he had better things to do than make sure all his schoolwork was perfect. Mom came home from the conferences and reported our most recent achievement test results: Eric was clearly brighter than his work demonstrated and was not working to his full capacity. I, however, was something of an anomaly. My test results said that my schoolwork was better than I was capable of doing—

the tests showed that I was "exceeding my potential." My mother, sensibly enough, thought this was priceless, though the joke completely escaped me at the time. I could only interpret it as an attempt to prove that I wasn't as smart or wonderful as I thought I was.

Eventually, of course, my potential caught up with my actual work, and by high school I had become quite skilled at multiple-choice exams, especially all those ETS-created life-determining aptitude/achievement/assessment tests. In one sense, this was a good thing, in that it gave me lots of options for college, but in another sense, it wasn't so great. We "smart" students always had our image to maintain—we couldn't risk looking like anything less than the best and the brightest, so we tended to overvalue grades and undervalue the kind of learning that would actually challenge us enough to risk those ever-so-important GPAs. (And the weird thing was, this attitude was almost entirely unconscious on our part.)

Academically, above all else, what I valued most about myself was my "efficiency"—being able to finish my work faster than anyone else, with the minimum of effort necessary to maintain that crucial GPA. Though occasionally other students would tell me I was a genius, I pooh-poohed the idea —I knew I was no genius. Geniuses had ideas, were creative, did amazing things no one else had thought of before. I was not a genius. What I was, I thought, was "bright." Being bright meant that I had a good memory, that I caught on to new things quickly, that schoolwork was easier for me than for most others.

Occasionally there was a hint that bright was maybe not

all that wonderful. One morning in physics, the teacher gave us a free period to review in small groups for an upcoming test. A classmate and I started reading through the relevant chapter, and I was startled to see how different our approaches were. I read through the text quickly, picking up enough of what was there to be able to guess correctly at how to plug values into the appropriate formula to come up with the right answers on the test.

Ben's method, though, was completely foreign to me. He'd read a sentence, and then he'd try to rephrase it in his own words to make sure he understood what it meant. Then he'd read the next sentence, and puzzle out its meaning. Okay, so he read things more slowly than I did. Big deal. But then he did something truly strange to me—he went back to the first sentence to see whether it still made sense in the context of the second sentence. And so he worked his way through the entire paragraph, phrase by phrase, back and forth until he felt he grasped its whole meaning thoroughly. At the end, he could do more than simply plug numbers into the right formula—he understood what the formula meant, and how it related to the physical behavior of real objects in the real world.

And what was my reaction? Did I suddenly comprehend what real learning was, as opposed to my usual recite-the-right-answer-for-a-good-grade efficiency? Not for an instant. I thought, "Wow, I'm sure glad I don't need to work that hard for my grades."

My education was not all rote and regurgitation, though. When I was eight, I fell off a bleacher and ended up in the hospital overnight for observation. Eventually, the doctors decided I'd torn a kidney, not seriously enough to need surgery, but enough to keep me home from school bedridden for a couple of weeks. My sister, three years younger, had just had her tonsils out (we came home from the hospital together), so my parents fixed us up in the same room so we'd at least have each other's company while we were stuck at home.

Even with our assignments from school and a portable television in the room, we were bored. Schoolwork didn't take that long, and the game shows and soap operas of those pre-cable days weren't all that engrossing. Eventually, Mom went to the library and brought home stacks of books, some to read to my sister, who was in kindergarten, and some for me to read myself. That was how I began to discover Robin Hood and Homer Price and the Mushroom Planet and Danny Dunn and the Arabian Nights and the Andrew Lang *Fairy Book* collections and the boundless worlds to be found in books.

From then on, I almost always had a library book with me at school. At first I read only during breaks or free reading periods or while waiting around for whatever was supposed to happen next. I remember one day sitting at the third grade reading group table, reading my library book while we waited for the teacher to join us, and a boy next to me asking how I could read and understand such a fat book. I slid it over so he could look at it, and he was incredulous. "That's just regular words," he said. "Anybody can read that."

Soon I started reading during teachers' lectures as well. I'd see when a teacher noticed me reading something

29

unrelated to the day's subject, so I'd pay just enough attention to what was going on in class that I could answer whatever question the teacher might throw at me. After failing to catch me out a couple of times, most would leave me free to read my books in peace.

My library books were my real education. Mom would take us to the library pretty much on demand, at least twice a month (our library system had a two-week loan period) and often more. My haul was typically 10–15 books at a time. I learned which librarians were the ones to ask for more titles similar to whatever my latest favorite was and which would tell me I wasn't allowed to read books beyond my age level. The best librarians, of course, were the ones who pushed me into genres I hadn't yet discovered.

When Mom couldn't get me to the library often enough, there was always the bookmobile, which showed up within bicycle range weekly. The bookmobile had the best librarians, too—they got to know their regular customers and would often bring something new they thought we might like.

I read all the Oz books. I read Nancy Drew and the Hardy Boys. I devoured fairy tales from all over the world. I read historical fiction. I discovered science fiction and moved rapidly through the juvenile science fiction to the adult science fiction, where I found Asimov and Bradbury and all kinds of speculative future worlds.

Nor did I only read fiction. I browsed encyclopedias and pored over atlases. I read biographies of people I'd never heard of before and histories of places and times never mentioned in school.

Without my even being aware of it, my "leisure" reading

developed my vocabulary and spelling. I was so used to seeing words in print that I instantly recognized when they were spelled wrong. I learned meaning from context and began to see how sentences flowed in good writing and in bad. By high school, I was rarely surprised in social studies or English classes. Whatever we studied, I'd usually already read about on my own.

I began to think of myself as a super-absorbent sponge, continuously soaking up ideas and information, taking things in and organizing it all in my mind for some indeterminate future occasion in distant adulthood, when all this seemingly random knowledge would somehow suddenly be wrung out of me to be of use to somebody somewhere.

Mixed in with the arrogance of my "smart" self was the sneaking suspicion that I was a fake, that I wasn't really the outstanding person that my teachers made me out to be. Sure, I could read exceptionally well, and I had an extraordinary knack for standardized tests and could phrase essays in ways that teachers approved, but I didn't know how to do anything *useful*.

Nor was I alone in that feeling. I remember a strange conversation with several classmates late in our senior year—at graduation practice, in fact—at our tracked high school. We "smart" ones were wistfully envious of the students in the non-college-bound tracks — we could see that they had a great deal more practical knowledge than we did, about things like taxes and insurance and getting and holding jobs. They had skills like typing and bookkeeping and drafting which could actually get them paid employment. We were naive about the world and we knew it. And we knew absolutely that we had to go to college because we simply weren't qualified to do anything else.

College began to crack the "smart" facade a bit. I took classes, got decent-enough grades in a nice liberal arts major. Two or three classes turned out to be outstanding, with professors who managed to make their subjects exciting and stimulating. I began to learn how to write, partly from one tiny English seminar but mostly from working as a reporter for the campus newspaper, where I learned how to interview and how to write to a deadline.

I graduated having no clue either what I wanted to do or what I was qualified for. (All that newspaper stuff had been just playing, as far as I was concerned then—real people weren't writers.) Because I had married and my husband had a job teaching high school physics and math at a private boarding school, I fell into a job teaching English and social studies—we were a package deal, it seemed, and to my knowledge, the school never made any effort to find out whether I was competent to do the job they'd hired me for.

I turned out to be an adequate teacher, but I never got over the feeling that I was only pretending to be a real teacher. I tried to avoid the most egregious problems I'd experienced in my own secondary school years, and I certainly wasn't the worst teacher in the school (though I was utterly shocked to learn that I was one student's favorite teacher). But only intermittently was I able to break through the daunting attitude that most of my students brought with them to class, that indifferent air of "I dare you to come up with anything that could interest me in the slightest."

Even if the students had been more interested, it was difficult fighting the essential "school-ness" of teaching. For my world history class, I was assigned the text I was to use (the principal told me that I could choose my own text the next year, once I had some experience)—the assigned book turned out to be the same dreary world history textbook I'd had during my own sophomore year in high school. Another teacher and I proposed a non-traditional approach to United States history for the next year, looking at events through the history of transportation systems—trade routes, canals, railroads, migration routes, highways and modern freeways, planes. We were excited about the idea—transportation provided an interesting filter through which to view American society. But our non-traditional proposal was denied—too non-traditional.

Two years of high school teaching was enough for me. I was happy to leave a job that felt like play-acting to me, though I still had no idea what kind of job really would suit me. It would take me another ten years to figure that out—but working that out is how I finally learned how to learn.

On Reading

Once I started reading for fun, reading was simply what I did. I was the stereotypical kid with her nose in a book. I read while walking to and from school. I read while I set the table for dinner. I read while watching TV. Thanks to the west-facing window in my room, during the summer I could read for hours after my ridiculously early parentally enforced bedtime, until I could no longer make out the letters on the page. On mornings when I didn't have to get up early for school and had finished whatever I'd been reading the previous night before total darkness hit, I'd pick a volume of the *Britannica Junior* at random from the bookcase next to my bed and browse for a while before I got up. Reading wasn't allowed at meals (meals were officially for family conversation), so I'd resort to surreptitiously reading milk cartons and cereal boxes and ketchup bottles if there was nothing else to read.

The nutritional content of random food products was not, of course, what I really looked for in my reading. What I sought in books—and often found—were worlds that were different from the one I lived in. My real world was an environment of routine, of going to school, of doing homework and household chores, and of getting up the next day and doing it all again. There were no choices in that world, other than deciding to finish my math homework before writing the English essay or reading that history chapter, or leaving the homework altogether until after the dinner dishes were done.

But I could grab a book and in just a few moments be in another world entirely, braving hazards with Dorothy Gale to outwit the Gnome King yet again, watching Susan Calvin create all those admirably superhuman robots, or empathizing with Lemuel Gulliver after his last voyage as he tried forlornly to find the Houyhnhnm in the ordinary horses in his stable. In books I found places I'd never been and places that never were and in my mind made them real. From books I learned how to face challenges and what people could be like and how to behave, and I experienced situations I'd never be in (or survive) in reality.

Naturally, when I had kids, I wanted them to have access to all those all those characters and worlds, too. I began to puzzle out how I learned to read and how from there I became an omnivorous reader. I found that I could remember a few incidents from before I could read, but not what being unable to read felt like. It's a process that I still ponder.

Reading is so much a part of my life that not only can I not remember what not reading felt like, but I can no longer even imagine myself not being able read. I think in text. No matter what I do or where I do it, a part of my mind is working on the text for it. If I'm listening to someone talk, that text-oriented part of my mind knows what the text of what they say looks like. It's not that I explicitly visualize all the individual letters and words in my head, but at some just-short-of-conscious level, all that text is there, scrolling past on my own personal mental TelePrompTer.

But it's worse than that. When I look at a tree, that text-mind of mine thinks "t-r-e-e." When I think of the color of that tree's leaves (and I *love* looking at tree leaves with all the varied greens that would never work next to each other in anything manmade), I don't first imagine what the color looks like. First I think "g-r-e-e-n"—in plain black letters on a neutral background, and then after my text-mind retrieves the word, I'll connect the word with the actual color.

What goes on in my head goes on in words. If I can't put it in words, I don't know what I'm thinking. Without words, I'm not sure I could think at all. Even strong emotions, the kind that overtake your consciousness with physical symptoms, like tears or goosebumps or giggles or giddiness, register at some level as "f-e-a-r" or "j-o-y."

But how did I get to this text-based mind of mine from learning to read with Dick and Jane?

My mother told me for years that I was taught to read with phonics. She's wrong, of course. I was of the generation of Boomers who learned to read with Dick and Jane and Sally and Spot and Puff, in the New Basic Readers Program, published by Scott, Foresman and Company from the 1930s through the 1960s. In the '50s, fully 80% of American first-graders were taught with the Basic Readers curriculum, which was a "whole-word" approach to reading. The texts used a limited vocabulary of simple and familiar words that were easy for children to recognize. Phonics were used to assist with the recognition of words, but the major emphasis was on the shape and context of words.

This "look-say" method of teaching reading was a huge innovation. The large, clear text and colorful illustrations, with stories that featured ordinary kids in everyday situations, were a radical change from the earlier dreary texts that lectured and preached more than entertained. But the new stories were themselves limited in their ability to engage new readers. Six-year-olds are not often gripped by 34-word narratives in which well over half of the words are "come," "and," "see," and "oh."

Many of us did not find phonics all that useful, either. "Sound it out" became a phrase I hated to hear, and since my mother was a firm believer in phonics, it was a phrase I heard often. The first instance I recall in which phonics was no help was in first grade. I was reading out loud to my mom and came upon a word I could not figure out: "s-n-o-w." I showed it to her and asked what it was, and she said, inevitably, "Sound it out." I had already tried to sound it out in my head, and it didn't make sense—it was "now" with an "s" stuck on the front, and I had no idea what a "snow" that rhymed with "now" and "cow" could be.

(Thirty years later when I first read Frank Smith's *Joining the Literacy Club*, I laughed out loud at his description of a computer analysis of 20,000 English words that showed that using the rules of phonics, combined with the multiple sounds that can be represented by letters and combinations of letters, a reader has only a 25% chance of pronouncing an unfamiliar word correctly.)

From the beginning of my reading career, I was a sight reader, using shape and context to figure out meaning. This meant that my reading got better as what I read became more interesting and meaningful. The better the stories, the more I wanted to read.

By the time my daughters were born, I believed in the power of narrative, and in the power of the five-step reading program I originally found on the Internet (and mentioned in *The Unschooling Handbook*):

1. Read to them.
2. Read to them.
3. Read to them.
4. Read to them.
5. Read to them.

And that is exactly what I did. I read to them. A lot. Afternoons and evenings. Before breakfast. At bedtime. On demand.

Sometimes they sat on my lap while I read. Sometimes they asked me to read while they drew or while they built something with blocks or LEGOs. Occasionally they would dig out dolls and stuffed animals and act out the stories as I read them. Sometimes they asked to hold the book and pointed at the parts they wanted me to read. If I was busy with something else, like fixing a meal, they might take a favorite book and pore over the pages on their own, just looking or copying the pictures, often with startling changes from the illustrator's original colors.

As my daughters reached school age, California was firmly in the midst of one of its periodic episodes of phonics mania, in which sight-based and "whole language" approaches to teaching reading are decried as ineffective and lacking rigor, and strict phonics programs are touted as the magical panacea that will bring all students up to grade level and raise all their standardized test scores to unprecedented heights. I told the girls that if they wanted to go to school, they could, but only after they could already read.

Kate, at five, appeared to be well on her way to reading. She knew the alphabet, could write and recognize her own name, and a few other simple words. She recognized all sorts of symbols when we were out—"stop" and "yield" signs, corporate logos and brand names on billboards—which clearly showed she was developing the skills she needed to become a reader. She would sit on the sofa, with Richard Scarry's *Best Word Book Ever!,* finding and reciting words for hours at a time.

Kate was an insatiable fiend for stories. We read fairy tales and mythology (she was the only six-year-old I've ever heard of who chose to be Medusa for Halloween) and Dr. Seuss. We read *Frog and Toad,* and *Amelia Bedelia,* and *Little Bear.* Gradually, the books got longer and the stories more complex, and the reading-out-loud sessions got to be an hour or longer at a time. Eventually, I had to make a new rule—I would only read five chapters in any one sitting. Kate complained, but she understood—after all, there wasn't any point in me reading out loud if I was so hoarse she couldn't hear me.

Fortunately, chapter books often have cliffhangers. And eventually there came a story that Kate just wasn't willing to wait until the next night to hear more of. The book disappeared into her room with her, and she became an independent reader.

She was eight and a half.

That wasn't so bad, I thought. Probably not as early as she'd have become an independent reader if she'd been in school, but there were advantages to learning to read on her own schedule. She didn't get bored with those too-dull readers I'd had to deal with in school, she thought of reading as something fun and interesting, and by the time she was nine, she could—and did—read just about anything that interested her. Above all, learning to read was something she had accomplished for herself, which gave her a level of confidence and faith in her own abilities I had never come close to at that age.

All in all, my experience with Kate gave me a lot of confidence that her younger sister would learn to read well just as easily. Not only did I know exactly how to help a child learn to read on her own, but Christie would have her older sister's example to learn from. She could take her time becoming a reader, and I wouldn't worry about it at all.

But Christie quickly drew my attention to the fact that she was a completely different person from her sister. I understood Kate very well, because she was much like me— we were both compulsive readers, we loved good stories in the same way, we both burrowed into those alternate universes we found in our reading. Kate had that same text-mind I did, except that hers was even better—she saw her "r-e-d" in *red* text and and her mental text for other words was embellished appropriately, as "v-i-n-e" would have vines winding around the letters or "c-l-o-u-d" would move and scatter just like a real cloud.

Christie was a hands-on character. Where Kate, faced with a new situation, would watch and observe to figure out what was going on, Christie wouldn't hesitate at all, but would jump right in. We found this to be literally true the first time we went to a swimming pool when she was about a year old. She saw the water, the water looked interesting, so in she went. For her parents, this approach was exhausting and frightening.

For Christie, this approach was often frustrating. Time after time, she'd see something to try that she did not yet have the motor skills or the coordination or the strength to do. No matter how hard she tried—and she would try again and again—she couldn't lift her own weight nor jump even half her height. By the time Christie became aware of reading as something she wanted to do, her sister was already an excellent reader who made it look easy. When it wasn't that easy for her, Christie decided that she wasn't as smart as Kate and switched her focus elsewhere.

She became a builder. She built fanciful LEGO constructions, sometimes connected to whatever that week's read-aloud was, sometimes completely original. She often concocted long, fanciful narratives for various dolls and stuffed animals who dwelled among the LEGOs.

She became a devotee of TV documentaries, of nature and science shows, and regaled us with explanations of the lives of cheetahs and leopards or the varieties of volcanoes and lava.

She learned huge amounts of information, much of which we had no idea where she picked up. She had a good intuitive understanding of arithmetic and geometry, mostly from several varieties of building toys, and of the mechanics of motion, from attempts to build small-scale siege weapons such as trebuchets and catapults for assaults on LEGO castles. But she still avoided reading.

When she was 9 or 10, she decided that she wanted formal lessons in reading. Okay, I thought, now she's ready—she just needs a little push and she'll pick it up just fine. So we went to a local bookstore and looked at reading books. She rejected several as looking too juvenile or frivolous, and after some serious consideration, she decided on *Teach Your Child to Read in 100 Easy Lessons.*

So we began the lessons. The novelty helped the first few lessons go well. But as we progressed through the book, Christie became more and more discouraged. "These stories are really stupid, Mom," she'd say. I quite agreed—the stories were incredibly dull, as most stories whose vocabularies are limited for pedagogical reasons tend to be. She could force herself to work through all the lessons, to read the annoying stories, but there was no pleasure in it for her, no sense of accomplishment, and there was no carryover from the lessons to reading anything else.

I suggested that if she didn't feel she was learning anything from the book, she should consider just quitting the lessons. "If the point of the lessons is to learn, and you're not learning from them, why keep on?" I asked. But she was determined. "I have to do these; I have to learn to read." And so we'd struggle through the next lesson or two, and then have the same discussion all over again. We finally abandoned *100 Easy Lessons* at about Lesson 63.

Finally, a few months past her twelfth birthday, Christie decided it was too inconvenient not being able to read. For several hours each day, she retreated into her room with stacks of American Girl books, and within a few weeks was reading on her own. By the time she was thirteen, she was a better reader than many other kids her age. She read to learn, when she needed to, though she also learned effectively from videos and observation. Though she never became the voracious reader her sister was, she frequently read for fun and was often shocked at how little some of her friends read.

Letting my daughters learn to read on their own schedule was for me the hardest part of our homeschooling experience. Undoubtedly, I could have pushed them both into reading earlier, but I'm convinced that doing so would have changed their views of reading and books, and would have dampened their natural curiosity and enthusiasm for learning. All too many kids in our society emerge from schools with books and learning defined as "school things" that they shouldn't have to bother with unless necessary for college or a job.

If I can learn with only two kids that no one method for learning to read works for every kid, how can it be so hard for our public schools to learn that lesson as well? How wasteful and destructive is a school system that expects all children to learn to read at the same age with the same method, when even just a little patience and flexibility could save millions of dollars in special education and remedial teaching expense? How hard would it be to cease labeling kids as inadequate or incapable of learning when the only problem is that they're on a different schedule from some mathematically "average" kid? Why do we seem to always want to view children through their weaknesses instead of through their strengths?

On Writing

THE ADVANTAGE OF HAVING SOMETHING TO SAY

There are any number of school subjects that seem to be taught in ways calculated to make students hate them, but the subject most often and most effectively taught in such a way is writing.

All through grade school, what I most wanted for school was a magic dictation machine that would take my thoughts and transcribe them in my own handwriting onto composition paper so that I didn't have to keep copying and recopying my essays each week.

There were quite specific rules for writing all those weekly essays (or themes or compositions——the term varied from year to year, though the form did not). Name, date, and subject were to be written in an upper corner, though the requisite corner could be left or right, depending on the teacher. The title was to be centered on the top line, with a line left blank before the body of the writing started. Three to five paragraphs were required, with each paragraph indented a half inch. There were to be no blank lines between paragraphs. Any mistake——spelling, punctuation, badly formed lettering ——was to be crossed out with a single horizontal line through it. Only three mistakes were allowed; if we made more than three mistakes, we were required to recopy everything onto a fresh sheet of paper.

Brain-hand coordination was never my strong suit, and my penmanship even then left much to be desired. (This could be hereditary——my father always had my mom retype his college notes the day he took them, because even he couldn't read his own handwriting after that. I suspect, though, that mostly my dad and I just never cared that much about penmanship.) I knew what I was trying to write——it was just that my fingers didn't cooperate. I was lucky to get through just one paragraph with only three mistakes; creating my final copy of any essay under those rules usually took four or five attempts.

Writing instruction when I was in school was a celebration of form over function. We were drilled on punctuation, with rules for using commas and distinguishing colons from semicolons. We learned the proper use of quotation marks and hyphens——and were discouraged from stooping to use the m-dash——which may be why I use it so much now.

We learned the parts of speech, about proper and improper nouns, transitive and intransitive verbs, and the differences between adjectives and adverbs. In junior high, we even had to memorize (and were tested on) a list of 23 prepositions——as though somehow we wouldn't be able to use "around," "over," "under," or "through" without explicit instruction. (My brother and sister were taught for a couple of years with a different system, using "class 1 words" and "class 2 words" instead of nouns and verbs and "helper words" for both adjectives and adverbs, which failed abjectly in its aim to simplify and clarify grammar instruction. I'm almost sorry I missed it by a year.)

Now and then, we got some minimal instruction on content. Outlines were the proper vehicles with which to create our content, and we spent a week or two each year in the upper elementary grades and junior high going over the fine details of creating proper outlines, making sure we had our upper- and lowercase Roman and arabic numerals and letters arranged in the proper order. (The existence of decimal outlines and less formal tools for organizing ideas was apparently information best left for adulthood, as was much advice on actual ideas to write about.)

Also of major importance were footnotes. Footnotes were the apotheosis of the emphasis on form, an arcane art made even more perplexing by the use of Latin abbreviations such as "ibid.," "op. cit.," and "loc. cit.," and by the difficulty of typing footnotes in those low-tech days when typewriters required the typist to guess at the amount of footnote space to allow.

My tenth grade English class provided a glimmer of hope with a unit on writing for different purposes. We were given assignments in class to write paragraphs in various styles: Write a paragraph describing how a strong emotion feels. Describe a tense or suspenseful situation. Advocate a political issue or candidate. Write a paragraph to persuade someone of something. Complain about an unsatisfactory business transaction and ask for redress.

One day, the teacher brought in grocery bags, and told us to write a physical description of the item we found in our assigned bag. Once we'd finished, we each passed our paper to another student, who had to sketch the item from our description. Instantly, most of us discovered how hard it was to draw a "long flat thingy with a little doohickey at one end that hooked up sideways to the other piece."

Those exercises were a revelation: different purposes and different audiences meant different styles of writing. And most astounding of all: writing was meant to communicate with its readers. I can't remember another time in school when it ever occurred to me that my writing could be used for something other than for the teacher to read and grade.

Unfortunately, it wasn't to last. The interesting, useful bits of writing yielded to the imperative of preparing for the next year's start of the college testing and admissions process, for which we needed to develop an extremely specialized—and virtually useless—skill: the timed essay.

The SAT, the ACT, the GED exam, high school exit exams, high school proficiency exams—nearly all include a 20- or 30-minute timed essay prompted by some inane question or quotation. "Some educators," for example, "believe that learning is a good thing. Do you agree or not? Give examples from your own experience."

The results can be as excruciating to read as to write. Take a look at *http://scienceblogs.com/challenge/* for the archived Blogger SAT Challenge, in which bloggers and blog readers were given the chance to write an SAT-style essay and have it graded by volunteers grading according to ETS standards. The whole project was prompted by a *New York Times* article ("Perfect's New Profile, Warts and All," Sept. 3, 2006) which scoffed at the quality of top-scoring essays released by the College Board. The idea of the Challenge was to test whether bloggers, who write short essays frequently, could do better at an SAT-type essay than the top-scoring high school test-takers. It turned out that the bloggers did no better than the high school students, managing to produce essays just as dull and lifeless.

As noted in the *Times* article, students who wrote longer essays scored better, those who wrote in cursive instead of printing scored better, and those who avoided a first-person voice scored better. The timed essay is the perfect test of form over function, allowing test-takers to produce writing with no intrinsic communicative function, writing that no one who is not paid to score it would be interested in reading.

By the time I got to college, I was an excellent writer— mechanically. I could spell words correctly almost without conscious thought, I was expert at the proper placement of punctuation marks, and unerring with subject-verb agreement. My main problem was that I had a terrible time figuring out *what* to write. The instant I had a sentence down on paper, I could see flaws that made it unacceptable. School writing instruction had not made me a writer—it had made me an editor. The problem was that I couldn't produce anything to edit. I could usually squeeze out enough of an essay or paper to get by with, but it was always a struggle.

Viral Learning

One tiny English seminar helped by encouraging us to read our work aloud to the others in the group. Reading aloud, we discovered, made any clunky sentences or gaps in logic glaringly obvious, and made it easy to discover what needed revising and expanding.

But none of my classes taught me as much about writing as working for the thrice-weekly college newspaper. I don't remember how I fell into it, or why someone as little fond of writing as I was would think I would enjoy it, but writing for the paper was a completely new experience for me—it made writing fun. We wrote to convey a specific set of facts to fit a limited amount of space, so the process was something like solving a jigsaw puzzle, except that we got to design the puzzle pieces before we tried fitting them into the overall framework.

For the first time, writing was a collaborative process for me. The editors read what I wrote and often made suggestions, copyeditors—usually whichever other writers happened to be free at the moment—caught typos and smoothed out phrasing, and everybody offered suggestions when anybody got stuck or couldn't think of the right word. We weren't writing to get a good grade or prove we were qualified for something else—we were just trying to fill that insatiable news hole with news worth reading three times a week.

Writing for the newspaper was writing under stress, but it was focused stress, aimed at achieving a concrete goal rather than meeting an arbitrary deadline. There was a purpose to what we did, and achieving that purpose taught us more about writing than our classes ever did.

School writing instruction has improved tremendously since my school days. Projects such as the Bay Area Writing Project, the National Writing Project, and their offshoots all over the country revolutionized the way writing was taught in schools. Decrying the overwhelming emphasis on mechanics that has been so prevalent in writing instruction, these programs advocated making writing meaningful to kids by giving them the means and skills to express their own ideas clearly and eloquently. Essentially, such programs provide a process, a sequence of steps from brainstorming through planning, creating a first draft, and revising to a final version, but the essential beginning of the process is helping the student figure out what she wants to say.

It was a revolutionary concept for most public schools—writing instruction that was not centered around spelling word lists or grammar rules but on helping kids become effective communicators, helping them articulate and communicate their own ideas. But there are problems with such programs: Teachers must devote far more time and energy with individual students, helping them develop their ideas. Grading is far more complex—multiple versions of essays cannot be evaluated as quickly or easily as multiple-choice questions, and the standards or rubrics for evaluation can be tricky. Should the writing be evaluated on the basis of the final version, on improvement from the early drafts or from previous projects? Should it be scored on a standard scale or in comparison with other students?

Process-oriented writing programs are often perceived the same way as whole-language reading programs—as fuzzy and ineffective, and not up to the rigor of strict standards-based curricula. They are not amenable to the kind of accountability testing in vogue these days, and all too many school districts give them up in favor of easier-to-manage mechanics-based programs.

As a homeschooling parent, though, I was convinced. I eschewed formal grammar lessons on the assumption that reading widely and often would give my daughters an intuitive feel for the formal structure of sentences. As they read more, they would develop a feel for what looked and sounded right and what didn't. We made sure they always had writing paper and utensils available, and bought them blank books regularly, in which they could keep journals and diaries for themselves. Our unbreakable rule was that no one else was ever to look into their journals unless and until specifically invited to by the writer. Privacy was absolutely guaranteed.

Another basic rule was that we would never answer any question about the spelling or meaning of a word with a command to "Look it up." We all knew where the dictionaries were and we all knew that everybody knew how to use them. When one of the girls asked how to spell a word, they were in the middle of a thought or a project they did not want to interrupt—answering their immediate question would help them more than making them prove to me that they could still use the same dictionary they had used the day before.

Neither girl was a voluminous writer. They were good at creating stories, which they told to us or to each other, or acted out, but that they seldom wrote them down did not alter the fact that they learned about how to structure stories, with beginnings and endings, and suspense in between.

But they did quite a bit of incidental writing. They wrote labels and captions for pictures they drew, thank-you notes for gifts they received, and copied recipes they wanted to try. As they got older and began to meet other homeschoolers at conferences and campouts, they discovered email, which rapidly developed from "Hi!!!! Whatcha doin'?" to multiple paragraphs of correspondence.

As they each reached 13 or 14, I gave them a copy of *The Elements of Style* for their own. (I admit it——I'm one of those people who love Strunk & White and try to reread it annually. Occasionally, I read Fowler's *Modern English Usage* just for fun, too.)

Best of all, they both had the technology I lacked when I wished for that magic dictation machine to write my compositions for me. When they were very young, they always had Mom to take dictation, to write down the captions or stories they wanted to accompany their drawings and paintings, of course. But when they were old enough to write on their own, computers made the mechanics almost as magical as that machine I'd always dreamed of——typos were easy to fix, and whole chunks of writing could be rearranged without trauma.

Essentially, writing was always a useful——and often entertaining——tool for my daughters. For them, it never became the drudgery my schooling had turned it into for me.

(That is, except for preparing for those timed SAT and GED essays when the time came.)

It's My House!

So Why Can't I Make All the Rules?

In *The Unschooling Handbook* I described three fundamental traits of an unschooling household:

- an environment conducive to exploration
- someone to serve as a learning model and facilitator
- trust that the child will learn

The first two are relatively easy: children are natural explorers and can find learning materials just about anywhere, and any parent interested unschooling is usually willing and eager to help their kids learn wherever their curiosity leads them, even if they occasionally feel overwhelmed.

But that third trait is a killer. Trust that your children will learn is isn't so hard while they're still toddlers. Toddlers are pure learning machines—learning to walk, learning language, learning how objects and people behave and ways to react, learning about how they themselves function. They're born unschoolers——it's exceedingly difficult to prevent children that age from learning.

But our society distrusts children: they're too young, too ignorant, too fragile to let them try too much on their own. Even when we want to trust our kids, it's hard to resist the mainstream social pressure to "protect" them, to provide strictures and limits (for their own good, of course). Trusting them also requires that we trust ourselves, often in the face of contrary advice from relatives, friends, and assorted other "experts," as well as those doubting interior voices that make us question our own judgment.

When my kids were born, my knowledge of child development and behavior was purely theoretical. In my own family, I was the oldest of three siblings born 18 months apart; I managed to grow up without much contact with younger kids or babies. As an adult, most of my friends had kids who were already in school or hadn't yet had any kids.

True to character, I resorted to books. I read lots of books on child development and behavior, and settled on a few staples for parenting advice: Dr. Spock seemed authoritative and sensible (not to mention that my mother said she had raised me according to Spock). Penelope Leach was warm and reassuring. I especially liked that the two of them frequently offered opposing advice——one warned against letting your infant getting chilly where the other cautioned against letting them get overheated. I added one more to the mix: T. Berry Brazelton added concern and care for the child's own feelings. I figured that among the three of them, I'd have appropriate advice for every conceivable situation I'd be likely to face——or at least, I'd have one certified expert to justify whatever I chose to do if my mom or some other critic questioned my judgment.

My parenting reference library worked quite well until a new expert began to intrude with wildly different ideas of her own. Kate turned out to be a far more reliable source of parenting expertise——not only were her lessons effective and impossible to ignore but they were absolutely tailored to her specific personality and needs.

One of her most memorable lessons occurred when she was in the midst of that transitional crawling stage when she scooted around on both hands, one knee, and one foot. She was incredibly fast, and one day when I turned for an instant to put a dish on a table a few feet away, I looked back to find her at my eye level——she had climbed halfway up the stairs that she'd never so much as glanced at before. Terrified, I gasped out loud, abruptly enough to startle her, and she fell. Fortunately, I was close enough to catch her before she fell far, but she was scared——though probably not as much as I had been——and in tears.

Eventually, we both calmed down. She returned to examining baseboards and furniture legs, while I skimmed through the newspaper. Within a few minutes, though, she giggled at me, and when I looked over at her, there she was on the stairs again, looking absolutely triumphant.

"Look at you!" I said. "What are you doing up there again?"

So I sat there on the stairs with her while she climbed up and down and up again, head first and feet first and sideways, always peeking to see whether I was watching, whether I could see how much fun she was having and what a pro she was becoming at negotiating those stairs.

It was around that same time that I came across a copy of John Holt's book on homeschooling, *Teach Your Own*. I sent right away for a sample issue of his newsletter, *Growing Without Schooling*, and after reading it, immediately subscribed, starting with #42. I also bought a complete set of back issues, which I perused avidly. Holt and his contributors didn't just talk about children's learning; they also talked about how the way children are often treated hinders their ability to learn and even their safety. There were many discussions in *GWS* about letting relatively young kids learn to use real paring knives or other household tools, on the theory that the sooner they knew how to use them properly, the safer they would be, along with advice on handling the adults who were appalled at the supposed danger *GWS*ers placed their kids in.

Coming on the heels of my afternoon on the stairs with Kate, this made perfect sense to me. At the time, I'd been planning to get a gate for the stairs, but now I reconsidered: To be sure, the gate would keep her off the stairs, but eventually, she'd figure out how to open it, probably on some busy day when I was so used to it being there that I wouldn't be paying enough attention, and without access to the stairs, she'd have had no practice using them. She could actually be *less* safe. We decided against the gate.

Suddenly I was reevaluating everything. Would this or that item help or hinder her learning? I was starting to wean her at the time—we didn't even own any bottles, but what about sippy cups? Wait, I thought. We want her to learn to handle a cup, so why protect her from small spills that wouldn't hurt her? We started with tiny cups only partly filled with water, and after a few attempts—and a few wet surprises —she knew how to hold a cup without spilling its contents and how to drink from it without dribbling down her chin.

As Kate—and later, Christie—grew older, this whole process became more explicit. We talked with them often about what they wanted to do, what the consequences might be, and whether what they wanted was possible or practical. We applied the philosophy of the sippy cup to scissors and blenders and money: the more practice one had using scissors and kitchen tools under supervision, the safer their use would be when—inevitably—we weren't there. We made sure they had a little bit of money for their own use as soon as they were old enough to grasp the concept, so that they could learn from their decisions with small amounts well before they had to face credit cards and rent and taxes, and a mistake could cost them far more than just the loss of a bit of cash.

The funny thing was, while all this discussion went on and our daughters learned to trust our advice, we learned to trust them and their abilities, too. Much to our surprise, they often came up with useful suggestions that hadn't occurred to us. In the process of helping them learn, we found that they gave just as much to that process as we did. We learned to take them seriously—most of the time—and they recognized that we did so. We were embarked on a collaborative adventure, working together learning, keeping the household functioning, living our lives.

Our parenting style, if you could call it that, was inextricably intertwined with our approach to learning, so much so that we couldn't have changed the one without drastically affecting the other. It's not that we never disagreed or argued or got annoyed with each other, but the basic foundation of respect, that fundamental trust we had in each other, never wavered.

One of the most interesting effects of the process was that we all started watching and listening to how other families interacted, and how most adults treat children. Restaurants, book stores, the grocery store, the mall, the zoo, and museums all provided glimpses into the dynamics of American families. All too often, we discovered, those dynamics were based on power. The parenting philosophy of Harry Wormwood, the dad in Roald Dahl's *Matilda*, is hyperbole, of course, but I'm not sure it exaggerates reality all that much: "I'm right. You're wrong. I'm smart. You're dumb. I'm big. You're little. And there's nothing you can do about it."

I've always suspected that many of the adult-child conversations in *Matilda* were reasonably faithful transcriptions of bits of real conversations Dahl actually heard. I may not have heard those exact words myself, but I've certainly heard that tone of contempt and derision from some parents. And because their kids learn from the adult models around them, that's the tone the kids eventually learn to use themselves.

Invariably on our excursions, we'd see a family who'd been out all day—the preschoolers exhausted and cranky and whining, and the parents frazzled and impatient. But as far as the parents were concerned, the kids' inability to cope any longer was willful, deliberately annoying, and more deserving of punishment than sympathy.

I learned to recognize that look of shocked dismay when it appeared on the girls' faces. I always dreaded looking to see what behavior they found shocking, but I knew they needed to know I was just as bothered it as they were. Often, what made us wince wasn't so much overtly abusive as it merely indicated the adults' lack of empathy with, and sometimes even contempt for, their own kids. The fact that comments like "How could you be so stupid?" or "Don't even think about saying one more word." seemed so routine was disheartening, to the point that every so often, we'd avoid public places for a while just so we wouldn't have to hear any of it.

We speculated about how parents could come to treat members of their own family so discourteously and disrespectfully, and concluded that such attitudes had to result from separation, from not being familiar with each other. When both parents work and the kids are in daycare or school most of the day, the time they spend together tends to be at the edges of the day, when everybody's rushing to get to where they need to be or is tired and hungry from a long day. Testy and irritable are not the best conditions for getting to know each other or learning to trust each other. Testy and irritable make it difficult even to like each other.

When we began to look for other homeschoolers to spend time with, we expected that they would have the same approach to family life that we did. But not everyone linked their parenting to their learning style as tightly as we did.

Most families seemed to assume that their kids needed lots of rules in order to know how to behave properly: No video games until after the laundry was folded. No sugar, ever. Always share all your toys. Only G-rated movies allowed for kids 12 and under. And dang, there were a lot of five- and six-year-olds with sippy cups.

Even worse were the few parents who not only had no rules, but apparently believed that modeling any kind of behavioral standards for their kids would be "stifling their creativity." These parents nodded approvingly as their darlings terrorized other kids, destroyed their own possessions and "borrowed" others, and expected instant obedience to their every command, only remarking, "Isn't it great that Ermintrude is so assertive?"

Many parents seemed not to notice or care that their edicts seemed arbitrary to their kids. One friend often told her kids that once they were adults, they'd get their chance to make all the rules. She told them she had had to do what her parents had told her when she was a kid, and now it was her turn. When they grew up and moved out into their own households, then they could make their own rules, but until then, she got to be the dictator.

Some of my strongest memories from my own childhood are incidents in which adults——sometimes my parents, sometimes teachers or other authority figures——acted in ways that were, to me, utterly arbitrary or mysterious. I remember a long discussion with my brother when we were eight and seven (I remember our ages because it was the summer we moved to a new city) about how bossy and unreasonable adults often were, and we swore we wouldn't be that way when we grew up.

I've tried hard to live up to that idea, though I'm sure my daughters would tell me I wasn't always successful, along with many times when my attempts to make sure they understood my whys and wherefores went on far too long and in far too much detail. There were even more than a few times when one or the other said, "Why can't you just punish us like other parents would so we don't have to *think* so hard about all this stuff?"

During her first semester in college, Christie called me one day, excited about her freshman psychology class, which that week was covering parenting styles. "Did you know there are three kinds of parenting?" she said, and went on to describe the conventional categories of authoritarian (my house, my rules, You Will Obey), permissive (kids are naturally good, so we shouldn't deny them anything or stifle their creativity), and authoritative (the perfect medium, firm but fair and affectionate).

At first, Christie thought I fell into the permissive category, since we never had strict rules about appropriate behavior or chores while they were growing up. (I had two explicit rules: 1. No food dishes may be left anywhere but in the kitchen. 2. If you want a parent to tuck you into bed, you have to keep a path to your bed clear of toys and other things we could trip over.) But she decided we hadn't been so indulgent as conventionally permissive parents would have been.

Clearly, we hadn't been authoritarian. But just as clearly, we hadn't taken that favored authoritative approach, either.

We lacked the firm but equitable rules-and-consequences expected of the wise authoritative parent. No corporal punishment, of course, but also no time-outs, no grounding, no withholding of toys or privileges. Christie eventually decided our family's style didn't really fit any of the conventional parenting paradigms.

So what were we? I considered the question for a bit and finally decided that our parenting process was collaborative. Our parenting was something we did *with* our kids instead of *to* them. By virtue of having been alive a couple (or three, in our case) decades longer than our children, we had more experience and knowledge about the world, so we could and did offer advice and support based on that experience. But we always tried to view ourselves not so much as parents training their children but as family members living together.

What this meant was that we tried to encourage everyone to be conscious and considerate of everyone else, to notice what needed doing and pitch in to help out. If the dishwasher needed unloading, whoever noticed it first could do it. Or if one of us was in the middle of a project, whether it was me writing or one of the girls reading or getting ready for a fencing tournament, the others might do more chores just to make things easier for the busy one.

In practice, of course, this often meant the house was messier than it might have been, or that sometimes one of us felt put upon if we had to ask someone to help clean house or sort laundry. But a simple request was usually all anybody needed to jump in to help, and by the time the girls reached their teens, they were as likely to nag us to do our share as we were to nag them.

Viral Learning

All too often, parents exercise power arbitrarily just because it's easy to do unthinkingly. But arbitrary power tends to perpetuate itself, to reinforce habits of obedience and resistance. Within a family, supposedly bound by love and affection, the use of arbitrary power distorts relationships and hampers learning. When parents demand respect from their children without giving it in return, they create conditions for resentment and subterfuge. When we treat our children as fully human, when we respect them and take them seriously as individuals, we make it possible for them to be the capable, self-reliant, interesting—and fun!—people we'd like them to be.

Accountability

When I was a kid, we——American society, that is——were excited about science and about the future. The Gemini and Apollo astronauts were celebrities, AT&T's Telstar satellite gave us broadcast television pictures live ("happening right now this very minute as you watch," as the excited reporters kept repeating), and medical advances like the new polio vaccines prompted visions of drastically longer lifespans.

It's hard not to laugh now at how enchanted we were with the miraculous transistor radios that you could carry around with you, with antennas no longer than a yard or so. Or how dazzled we were at the concept of the often-promised and somehow never delivered videophone that the phone company (there was essentially only the one, then) kept dangling as an example of what would be coming in the future.

Viral Learning

All that technological change had been developing for some decades, of course, but it exploded into the consciousness of the American public with the launch of the Soviet Sputnik satellite. Suddenly American technological hegemony was in doubt and education became an important component of national defense. In 1960, Congress passed the National Defense Education Act, which, with its emphasis on federal funding for science and mathematics to allow the U.S. to "catch up" with those pesky Soviets, jump-started a continuing series of fixes for the ills of our school system.

We don't seem ever to settle on the exact root of the problem, though. Sometimes it's the teachers, who aren't properly credentialed, sometimes it's the schools, which have too much money or too little or are too bureaucratic, and sometimes it's the curriculum, which isn't rigorous enough or is too inflexible. Sometimes it's the students, who are too lazy and unfocused or just don't try hard enough.

In 1994, I got to wallow in a orgy of education reform ideas as the representative of the HomeSchool Association of California at what was called the California Education Summit. This conclave was the creation of California's then-Speaker of the Assembly Willie Brown and was announced as an opportunity for the state's legislators to gather ideas for reforming the state's faltering school systems.

Every possible interest group was represented: school administrators, textbook publishers, teachers' unions, school boards, economists, education professors, law enforcement officials, private school directors, even our tiny sprinkling of homeschoolers. There were more than 600 attendees, of whom about 40 gave formal presentations and nearly 150 served on seven panels over the two days of the festivities. Brown put on an impressive show: we heard from such luminaries as Marian Wright Edelman of the Children's Defense Fund; Robert Reich, then U.S. Secretary of Labor; James Comer of Yale's Child Development Program; and Gray Davis, then state controller and soon-to-be (briefly) governor of California. We received little goodie bags filled with tokens from the corporate sponsors (Taco Bell, Pepsi-Cola of California, the California Manufacturers Association, Southern California Edison, and the Wine Institute, among others) who helped pay for the whole shebang.

The formal presentations focused on the changing demographics of the state's school population, on workforce preparation and the state's economy, on teacher preparation and retention, on education technology, on standards and testing, on violence in schools, on school finance, and——oh, yes——on "Children and Learning: factors that affect a child's ability to learn."

That last was the panel I sat on. After the half-dozen experts assigned to the topic gave their testimony, the two dozen of us sitting on the panel got to take turns——as Speaker Brown controlled our microphones——responding to what those experts had to say. With only a minute or two for each panelist in this "discussion," most didn't bother to speak to the topic but opted for little mini-rants on the subjects dear to the organizations they represented.

As a mere homeschooler representing the group that annually spent the least amount of money lobbying the state legislature (we spent a dollar a year on our professional lobbyist, who also just happened to be a homeschooling dad), my microphone was never turned on. But I still know what I would have said:

> One of the first things we homeschooling parents learn from helping our kids learn is that there is something that is far more important to learning than all the inputs we're talking about here at this summit. *Where are the students?* How can any long-term solutions for educating students in our state have any hope for success without at least some participation by the people on whose behalf we're ostensibly making all this effort? Beyond holding teachers accountable to the schools and schools accountable to the state's taxpayers, aren't we ultimately accountable to our children? *Why have our children no voice in this?*

Our children, of course, don't pay lobbyists or bundle campaign contributions.

That whole issue of accountability messes up many homeschooling parents as they try to figure out how and what their kids should learn. Let's say you're just starting out homeschooling your six-year-old, and you're determined to do a good job. So you take a look around the web and find your state's content standards and discover something like this (from the California English-Language Arts Content Standards for first grade):

> Students write clear and coherent sentences and paragraphs that develop a central idea. Their writing shows they consider the audience and purpose. Students progress through the stages of the writing process (e.g., prewriting, drafting, revising, editing successive versions).

and

> Students write compositions that describe and explain familiar objects, events, and experiences. Student writing demonstrates a command of standard American English and the drafting, research, and organizational strategies . . .

Uh, right. You're not too sure your 15-year-old nephew could manage that, let alone your six-year-old daughter. Maybe instead you'll look at social studies, thinking you can talk with her about concepts like "neighborhood" and "town." So you take a look at the California History-Social Science Content Standards for first grade:

> . . . Students describe the human characteristics of familiar places and the varied backgrounds of American citizens and residents in those places.
>
> 1. Recognize the ways in which they are all part of the same community, sharing principles, goals, and traditions despite their varied ancestry; the forms of diversity in their school and community; and the benefits and challenges of a diverse population.
>
> 2. Understand the ways in which American Indians and immigrants have helped define Californian and American culture.
>
> 3. Compare the beliefs, customs, ceremonies, traditions, and social practices of the varied cultures, drawing from folklore. . .

Perhaps it's just the bureaucratic nature of the state standards that makes them sound as though they could just as easily be used by the local community college. So you look for something a bit less formal to get you started, such as the

Viral Learning

World Book Encyclopedia's "Typical Course of Study" for first grade:

- **Social Studies**
  - Holidays, traditions, and customs
  - Our American heritage
  - Different cultures at different times
  - Family, school, neighborhood, community
  - Farm and zoo
  - Neighborhood helpers
  - Jobs and careers
  - Social skills and responsibilities
  - Basic geography terms
  - Making and reading a simple neighborhood map
- **Language Arts**
  - Reading
  - Phonetic analysis
  - Structural analysis
  - Establishing sight vocabulary
  - Reading informally: names, labels, signs
  - Simple pantomimes and dramatic play
  - Creating stories and poems
  - Telling favorite stories
  - Organizing ideas and impressions
  - Enunciation and pronunciation
  - Presenting information orally, in sequence and with clarity
  - Book reports and critiques
  - Discussion skills: taking part in group discussion
  - Beginning dictionary skills: alphabetizing
  - Beginning spelling
  - Beginning grammar: nouns, verbs, adjectives
  - Introduction to punctuation and capitalization
  - Manuscript handwriting
  - Handling books
  - Using table of contents
  - Development of a class newspaper

That's on the right planet, at least. It sounds like things some six-year-olds might actually do from time to time. But how do you translate it all to homeschooling? "Susie, sit down now—it's time to study your social skills and responsibilities." Even the friendlier *World Book* suggestions can be daunting and intimidating. It's no wonder so many new homeschooling parents trying to be responsible educators for their kids are quickly discouraged and overwhelmed.

What those who persevere soon discover, though, is that standards and formal curriculum can also be limiting as they attempt to be comprehensive. With a huge, defined body of material to cover, there's not much freedom to wander afield, to follow threads into subjects not scheduled to be covered that week, that month, or that year. It's all too easy for the structure to become a floor and ceiling within which to confine the content, instead of a framework around which to organize whatever material intrigues and fascinates our kids, a framework that can be filled in with bits and pieces in any order that suits our kids' learning style and pace.

But without that formal structure, some homeschooling parents feel lost. Without a formal plan, created in advance and adhered to faithfully, how will they know how well their kids are doing? How can they determine whether they're doing a good job educating their children? How can they prove that their kids are keeping up with schooled kids, that they'll be qualified for college or the job market?

I was lucky in that regard, having been a high school teacher for those two years a decade before my first daughter was born. One aspect of that experience that fascinated me was what a waste of time all the tests I ever gave seemed to be.

Viral Learning

Over those four semesters I taught freshman English, western American literature, U.S. history, world history, and American government, and in all of those classes, no student ever surprised me with test results radically different from the rest of the work they'd done for the class. (There was the one term paper that was clearly an excerpt from a published book, but that was a different matter entirely.) The point—and it's one I've confirmed with many teachers since then—is that most teachers are keenly aware of how their students are doing in their classes without needing exams to tell them.

It's a rare homeschooling parent who lacks the same knowledge and awareness of how her own kids learn, of what their strengths and weaknesses are, of what fascinates them and what leaves them bored out of their skulls. Most homeschoolers who opt for testing to tell them how their kids are doing discover that the tests tell them pretty much what they already knew about them.

It's difficult for most of us to avoid tests, though. State laws may mandate testing at certain ages, some employers use standardized tests in their hiring process, and the whole college admissions process is full of opportunities to learn to think in the Educational Testing Service way. For many homeschoolers, performing well on standardized tests can be much the least troublesome way to meet admissions or job requirements.

With standardized tests used and overused so ubiquitously now, it's tricky for homeschoolers to keep tests in proper perspective. When high school students take the SAT three or four or even more times in order to maximize their scores and grade school students spend a month or more preparing for the latest incarnation of accountability testing to prove their schools aren't "wasting" taxpayer money, it's clear our society has not managed to keep such tests in perspective.

(The testing and retesting mandated by the No Child Left Behind Act always puts me in mind of an insane medical center where the medics keep taking the patients' temperatures:

"This one's still running a fever, Doctor."

"Ah, that's not good, Nurse. Take his temperature again."

"Nope, still feverish, Doc."

"Gee, this patient isn't improving at all. If his temperature isn't down enough next time, we'll have to try reducing the amount of food he's getting. And if it stays high much longer after that, we may have to replace you, Nurse, and bring in a different nurse to take his temperature.")

With the right attitude, tests can be fun. As games or puzzles, they can even be interesting. But no matter how challenging figuring out the thinking of test designers is, or how useful test-taking skills can be for a limited few years of life, the time spent learning to take standardized tests is time spent away from real learning. Whether students in school or unschoolers at home, our kids lose with the emphasis on test results.

Test prep steals time from "non-essential" learning—frivolities like music and art and lab work yield to the imperatives of vocabulary-building and sentence completions, to history and science reduced to factoids that can be encompassed in multiple-choice questions, and to learning reduced to the accumulations of trivia I think of as "Jeopardy knowledge."

Back at that Education Summit I went to, one of the best (and worst) stories was one told by a man named Rafe Esquith, who'd won a couple of national teaching awards. He told how he'd struggled to teach junior high English at an inner-city Los Angeles school, trying to figure out a way to get his functionally illiterate students excited about reading. He eventually hit on a radical approach: he got his students acting out *Macbeth*. Somehow, the Elizabethan language and the murderous plot grabbed his students. They pieced together costumes for themselves, helped each other learn lines, and somehow discovered they liked Shakespeare and theater and even reading. Esquith's administrators weren't so enchanted, though—they shut the program down, saying (and Esquith swore this was a direct quote) "We want you to do something academic."

"Something academic" undoubtedly meant something "objective,"—something easily testable, scorable with Scantron cards and #2 pencils, something that could be studied for by rote memorization and forgotten as soon as the testing was over, except for the trace memory of learning as drudgery, as irritation to be avoided whenever possible.

My daughters took somewhat different approaches to testing, due to their differing goals. Kate, applying to acting schools which were mostly interested in her performance in auditions, only needed some kind of outside proof of a high school diploma. She got herself a GED preparation book, took a month or two to work through it, aced the tests, and submitted her GED scores to her schools. Aside from a bit of minor resentment, she was barely distracted from reading her plays and acting in community theater.

For Christie, applying to conventional colleges, the whole process was far more onerous, complicated by the need to build a relatively conventional transcript for the NCAA Clearinghouse, since she intended to complete in intercollegiate athletics. She slogged her way through algebra and geometry and algebra 2 texts that gave her what she needed for both her NCAA core courses and minimum SAT score requirements, but it was a struggle the whole way. She ranted regularly about spending so much time and energy on material she knew she would forget, procrastinated working on it, complained that I didn't force her to get it done, and resisted doing it when—at her own request—I nagged her about it.

The worst effect of Christie's test preparation was that it made her begin to believe that learning was supposed to be hard. She compared the hours her teammates at the fencing club spent on homework while she read whatever interested her. She started to think that perhaps she didn't deserve to go to college because the bulk of what she had learned her whole life had been fun to learn, that it didn't count as real education because it hadn't been a struggle the way most of her high school-level math had been. She left for college convinced that she was completely unprepared, and it took her most of her freshman year to discover that, despite a few gaps here and there in her knowledge, her serious-but-fun approach to learning worked better than the "slogging through" style she'd disliked so much.

I'm not allowed to say I told her so, though.

Duh.

What Homeschoolers Have Known for Years

When we began our homeschooling, we had no particular plan for the whole process. I'd spent years telling relatives that "We're just playing things by ear. We'll see how we all do and decide whether it's working after we've been homeschooling for a while." Though I was never as equivocal about the decision to homeschool as that sounded, I was always less certain about the methods we would use.

But during their infant and toddler years, my daughters thoroughly reinforced my instinct to continually question what we were doing. Almost always, when we thought about what we needed to do next, we asked "Why?" or "Why not?" (And those few times that I neglected to ask those questions, one or both of the girls would inevitably ask it for me.)

Because of this, our curriculum over the years didn't look much like a conventional school program. Take social studies, for example. When I was in school, social studies had been a series of courses repeated in more depth and detail. In the primary grades, social studies consisted mostly of a bit about maps, along with the commemoration of major holidays with appropriately themed worksheets and construction paper decorations. In fourth grade, we got more serious with state history (which in California usually means building a model of one of the 21 missions the Spanish established along the coast in the 18th century, a tradition so ingrained that school supply stores carry mission kits, though in my day we usually only used sugar cubes for our imitation adobe). Fifth grade was American history, sixth grade was Latin American geography and history, seventh grade was a conglomeration of Greek and Roman mythology and art and music appreciation called "world cultures," and eighth grade was American history and government. High school continued the recycling of topics with ninth-grade geography, tenth-grade world history, eleventh-grade American history (yet again, though this time I think we made it past the Civil War and all the way to the Depression), and twelfth grade civics, known then at my school as "Government and American Problems."

My daughters' social studies program was another matter entirely. We did manage some relatively formal study of California history, but that was as part of the preparation for a couple of overnight living history excursions to Sutter's Fort with our local support group. Otherwise, our explorations of history and geography and sociology were utterly haphazard, prompted by trips we took, by current events, or by movies and documentaries we happened to see, and mixed up inextricably with literature, theater, and the history of science.

Viral Learning

Long binges of Elizabethan history were originally prompted by a PBS broadcast of the Lincoln Center production of *The Comedy of Errors*, featuring the Flying Karamazov Brothers. When their first exposure to Shakespeare included jugglers, acrobats, puppets, klezmer music, and a drag queen, Kate and Christie were unlikely to view Shakespeare's plays as boring or intimidating. Kate found biographies of Elizabeth I and the other Tudor monarchs, and eventually talked us into the first of several years of annual treks to local and regional Renaissance faires.

We watched the Branagh *Much Ado About Nothing* and *Henry V*, which, with a little help from *Mythbusters*, led Christie into building small trebuchets with which to lay siege to her LEGO and Kapla castles. In our quest for new versions of Shakespeare plays, we jumped from the Olivier *Richard III* to the kitschy but fun Roger Corman-Vincent Price *Tower of London* to Ian McKellan's *Richard III* (which led to another whole line of exploration into World War II and 20th century American and world history) and Al Pacino's *Looking for Richard*.

The reality was far more convoluted, winding from one era and subject to another and another. The girls ended up knowing quite a lot about some periods and areas of the world and not much about others, but they had a good sense of chronology and could fit new knowledge into what they already knew despite the lack of a strictly sequential approach to learning it all.

More than that, though, what they learned, they learned because they cared about it enough to keep learning more. They dug into the subjects that interested them in detail far beyond what school textbooks would have provided them, and what they learned, they *knew*—they didn't need to have their knowledge reinforced by repetition every few years.

Wow, I think now—it actually worked. I could say I always knew it would, but it would be more accurate to say that I always *hoped* it would. There was probably a part of me that never doubted what I was doing, that always believed that my daughters were getting the best education they could possibly have, that just looking at what they spent their time on demonstrated that our approach to learning was working perfectly. There may well have been a part of my mind with that kind of confidence, but that part was buried deep beneath the doubt and worry and second-guessing that torment most homeschooling parents.

To keep my uncertainty at bay, I began collecting what I've come to think of as "duh" research. Duh research consists of studies that essentially confirm what I've seen in my own kids and dozens of other homeschooled kids. It's academic research that is the somewhat more rigorous counterpart to our anecdotal experiences. Is it scientific proof that unschooling works? Probably not. But it's certainly evidence that supports the conclusion that we're on the right track, that what cognitive pyschologists are learning about how our minds function is consistent with what we do as unschoolers. (And it certainly never hurts to have such studies available to throw at skeptical relatives and friends.)

One of the areas of study that really strikes home with me is the potentially adverse effect of praise. (*New York Magazine* had a great article on this in their February 2007 issue, in "How Not to Talk to Your Kids," by Po Bronson.) Most parents and teachers are good at couching negative criticism narrowly, so that it's directed at specific behaviors rather than to the whole individual. We know to say, "Lighting firecrackers in the kitchen is a stupid and dangerous thing to do" instead of "Why are you such an idiot?"

But we don't often think about the effects of positive comments in the same way. When our child has done something we're pleased with or proud of, we think nothing of saying, "You're so smart and clever. You're just amazing." It doesn't occur to us that such generalized compliments could be just as damaging as generalized negative remarks. (Not to mention that we really like complimenting our kids when they do well. After all, isn't that practically complimenting ourselves as parents, too?)

It turns out, though, that kids who are regularly told they are smart often start to play things safe, to refrain from trying new or challenging things. If they are so smart, the reasoning goes, they should be able to perform the new or challenging test easily. If they can't, then that must mean that they aren't really smart and that because they aren't really smart, there's no point to even trying.

The *New York* article describes an experiment conducted by Columbia University psychologist Carol Dweck with New York fifth-graders. Individual students were given a series of fairly easy nonverbal puzzles to solve, told how they scored on solving them, and then told either "You must be smart at this" or "You must have worked really hard."

Then for the next test, the students got to choose between an easy test similar to the first group of puzzles or a harder test that they could learn a lot from by trying. A majority of the students who had been told they were smart opted for the easier test, while 90 percent of those who'd been told they'd worked hard chose to try the more challenging puzzles.

In the next stage, all the students were given a much more difficult test, targeted for seventh graders, though they weren't told this. The "smart" students interpreted their difficulty with this test as evidence that they weren't truly smart, while the "hard-working" students mostly thought they just needed to put more effort into considering possible solutions.

Finally, both groups were given a group of easy puzzles like the first test. The "hard workers" improved on their original scores by about 30% while the "smart" students' scores dropped by about 20%.

I found myself flashing back uncomfortably to my own school days while I read this article——in effect, I had been one of those "smart" kids, told often by my parents and by teachers——and by that whole alphabet soup of standardized tests over the years——that I was smart. And my reaction was, from the perspective of this article, entirely unsurprising: I concentrated on those subjects that were already easy for me and opted out of any challenges that might endanger that perception of myself as "bright."

I can see the same pattern with my daughters, too. Whether it was partly due to how we as parents treated them partly to how they viewed each other and themselves, and partly simply the four-year difference in their ages, Kate was perceived as the more intellectual "smarter" child while Christie was the more hands-on, persistent one. And sure enough, Kate was one who was more easily discouraged by difficult tasks. Christie, on the other hand, occasionally even alarmed us with her refusals to give up on anything she'd decided she could and would do.

There's another hazard to praise, too—a side-effect of all the various self-esteem programs of the past couple of decades. Most kids are pretty good at sensing whether praise is genuine or not, and many schoolkids learn early that they get praised when they've reached their limits. Most come to view praise as something given to those who aren't "smart," in an attempt to keep them from feeling bad about themselves, so that the actual effect of such praise is the opposite of what is intended by it.

It's also starting to look like actually being smart isn't any more useful than being told you're smart. That's a flip way to put it, but research by Martin Seligman and Angela Duckworth appears to show that self-discipline is a better predictor of academic performance than IQ.* They studied eighth graders over two years, looking at grades, IQ scores, the number of hours spent on homework, as well as self-, parent, and teacher evaluations of self-discipline. It turned out that both IQ and self-discipline correlated with grades, but that self-discipline was far more influential than IQ. Students with high self-discipline scores earned higher grades than those with with high IQs only, and those with lower self-discipline scores earner lower grades than students with low IQs. Essentially, working hard pays off more than mere brains.

Nor is it just brain-smarts that are outdone by work. The same principle appears to hold for activities like sports, too. A psychologist named Anders Ericsson, at Florida State

* Duckworth, A.L., and Seligman, M.E.P. (2005). Self-discipline outdoes IQ in predicting academic performance of adolescents. Psychological Science. 16(12), 939–944.

DUH.

University, studies what he calls "expert performers," trying to understand what makes the difference between people who are good at something and those who are exceptional. Take fencing, for example—what differentiates the top two or three dozen nationally ranked fencers from the two or three very top fencers who consistently make world teams for several years running? (Or, if you prefer a more common example, what made Michael Jordan Michael Jordan?)

The big difference appears to be what Ericsson calls "deliberate practice." This is not mere repetition, shooting 10,000 free throws or performing 10,000 saber head cuts. It's practice with specific goals for improving technique and immediate feedback for evaluating progress toward the goals. In other words, talent is overrated. Talent certainly helps, but between two equally talented individuals, the one who devotes hours and energy to deliberate practice will be the star performer, and an average athlete or artist who engages in deliberate practice will probably outperform a more naturally talented individual who doesn't put in the work.

There's a logical corollary to Ericsson's work, too: when you're deciding what to do with your life, you should do something you love, simply because you'll *want* to work hard enough at it that you will get to be very good at it.

One of my favorite bits of duh research is actually a major clinical report from the American Academy of Pediatrics in October 2006: "The Importance of Play in Promoting Healthy Child Development and Maintaining Strong Parent-Child Bonds." The paper's abstract says:

Play is essential to development as it
contributes to the cognitive, physical, social,
and emotional well-being of children and
youth. Play also offers an ideal opportunity for
parents to engage fully with their children.
Despite the benefits derived from play for both
children and parents, time for free play has
been markedly reduced for some children. This
report addresses a variety of factors that have
reduced play, including a hurried lifestyle,
changes in family structure, and increased
attention to academics and enrichment
activities at the expense of recess or free child-
centered play. This report offers guidelines on
how pediatricians can advocate for children by
helping families, school systems, and
communities consider how best to ensure play
is protected as they seek the balance in
children's lives to create the optimal
development milieu.

Most homeschoolers have heard—and made—most of
the AAP's arguments before, about how too many children
today are over-scheduled, how there is so much pressure for
children to excel in every field in order to build the
appropriate resume for getting into the right college, and
lamenting how limited kids today are in opportunities to
simply be and do for now instead of always preparing for
those important future goals. The AAP's got a tough battle on
its hands, though—it's not just teachers and school systems
and parents who need to be reached, but many kids as well.

When Kate was 16, she and a couple of friends had a chat
with the fencing coach of an Ivy League university about what
he and his school looked for in students applying for
admission there. He asked them about their grades and their
extracurricular activities, and one girl explained that in

addition to her high GPA in the International Baccalaureate program and top SAT scores and her national ranking in fencing, she was in her school's marching band and on the debate team and student council and . . . "Stop!" he said. "That's too much. If you've got good grades and your sport, you really should have only one other solid extracurricular. Otherwise, it looks like you're not really interested in anything but collecting items to add to your resume." The girl was so focused on her achievements that she was mystified by this, though Kate and her other friend were relieved—they liked the idea that it was okay to take enough time to enjoy their *now* instead of constantly focusing on the future.

And then there's all the electronic technology we can play with today. As one who enjoys good movies and television, and has seen how watching both, in addition to playing computer games, has sparked my kids' interests, I was definitely predisposed to favor Steven Johnson's arguments in his book *Everything Bad Is Good For You.* The subtitle pretty well summarizes his contention: "How Today's Popular Culture Is Actually Making Us Smarter." Johnson cites examples from different eras of television, videogames, and the Internet to argue for their increasing complexity over the years. (For one thing, it's hilarious to compare his little graphs of the plotlines of *Dragnet* to those of *The Sopranos.*)

Johnson describes the ways people learn from video games and the Internet, how they become adept at learning by exploring their environments. Gamers don't sit down and read manuals—they sit down at their console and start clicking to see what happens and which bits on the screen activate game functions. They literally learn by doing.

Viral Learning

It's almost enough to make you believe that conventional education could be making itself obsolete.

I've certainly found that I'm far less patient than I once was with classroom-based learning. I don't want to wait around for the instructor to catch up with my interests, I don't want to use a syllabus someone else has created. I want to learn what I want to learn, and I want to learn things my way. Partly, of course, this is a matter of age—in my fifties, I know a great deal more about what I know and what I don't and how I learn than I did 30 or 40 years ago.

But I find it difficult to believe that the lecture-recall models of learning so prevalent in schools can survive in the face of the kinds of learning we can do on our own these days. Kids who design and maintain their own blogs or websites aren't going to sit still for lectures on HTML and CSS, and those who've explored social theory in *Sim City* or *Civilization* —or devoured political blogs and current events—may well find high school social studies a bit simplistic.

Finally, we come to the best bit of all my duh research. After years of arguing with unschooling skeptics about how kids will, too, learn things even if we don't force them and that learning is, too, supposed to be fun, I've found some research showing that's literally true. Irving Biederman, a USC neuroscientist, has discovered, using functional MRIs, that human brains release natural opioids at the moment we comprehend a new concept.[*] Apparently, the more we learn, the more we want to learn. We are, in fact, addicted to the acquisition of new knowledge.

[*] Biederman, I., & Vessel, E. A. (2006). Perceptual Pleasure and the Brain. *American Scientist, 94*, 249-255.

Happily Ever After

THE JOYS OF AMBIGUITY, DOUBT, AND UNCERTAINTY

We homeschooling parents—most of us—are enthusiastic promoters of homeschooling. Especially when we're first starting out, we're tireless answerers of questions and explainers of all our whys and hows and ends. Give us an in-law, a neighbor, or a store clerk, and we're full of information about how wonderful homeschooling is, how it frees our kids' imaginations and lets them find their best selves.

Best of all, homeschooling improves our family life. We get to know each other far better than if the kids were off at school all day. Siblings learn to get along with each other—even widely spaced siblings willingly spend time playing together and helping each other learn. Parents and kids get along, too—we discuss current events and the books we read and handle behavioral issues before they become problems.

That's what we tell all the non-homeschoolers, anyway. Even among other homeschoolers, we're often leery of discussing problems. Sure, we'll talk about looking for a better way to learn fractions or ask for advice about finding a Spanish tutor. But serious problems? Your ten-year-old doesn't speak outside the house or your teen can't handle basic arithmetic calculations? How can that be when everybody else seems to homeschool so easily? If your homeschooling life isn't so smooth and calm, maybe it's because you're not doing it right. Maybe you're just not any good at homeschooling.

Sometimes we're so invested in the wonderfulness of homeschooling that we expect it to solve every possible problem. We let our expectations exceed reality and see any trouble as a sign that we're not good enough, forgetting that if our kids were in school, we'd be worrying about their teachers or their test scores or even some of the same things we worry about when we're homeschooling. Not everything has to do with our educational choices.

For years, I've joked about parental panic attacks and how easy it is to let them disrupt our lives unnecessarily. It's only in recent years, though, that I've started to talk much about my own homeschooling panic attack, when I suddenly doubted everything I'd ever believed about homeschooling. I was irresponsible and clueless, I thought. I was recklessly risking my daughters' well-being, jeopardizing their entire future. And I couldn't say a word about it—I'd submitted the final revisions to *The Homeschooling Handbook* a few weeks earlier. My first book was about to make me a very public advocate for homeschooling, and there I was, seriously considering enrolling my kids in public school so we could be conventionally normal. What on earth was I to do?

Fortunately, I didn't do anything, which was a bit of advice I found in the printed edition of *The Homeschooling Handbook* when my author copies showed up at my door:

> Take a deep breath, and count to 10 (or 20 or 50 or 100 or 10,000). Don't make any drastic changes in your lives for a few days—wait to see if the worry just evaporates.

That's exactly what my worry did—it just evaporated. Suddenly everything was okay again. I was saved the public humiliation of repudiating my book and the financial hardship of repaying my long-spent book advance. As I flipped through the pages of the brand new books, I even found another piece of advice I often followed over the next ten years:

> Reread a favorite homeschooling book or article. Sometimes you'll find you just needed to be reminded of the ideas that got you started homeschooling in the first place.

It's embarrassing to think about how often I found myself referring to my own books as my daughters grew older. But once I'd finished all the editing and proofing and a few months had passed, I'd forgotten much of what I'd written. More than once, I'd read an article in a new homeschooling magazine or newsletter and think, "Wow, that's a good idea," only to find at the end that I'd not recognized an excerpt from my own book.

What I'd written was theory, based on what I'd learned from other homeschoolers who'd contributed to the book and from those we'd come to know during our first four or five years of homeschooling. But it took more years of experience, living and learning and doing, for that theory to become real knowledge.

Along the way, I was not the only one who doubted. Both of my daughters had stretches when they questioned whether homeschooling was worth the effort, when they wondered whether a conventional school might be easier or better or less risky. Both also occasionally thought school might be easier because they were tired of being different.

Most homeschooled kids suffer through the neighborhood kids' quizzes ("How will you ever be smart if you don't go to school?") and the too-frequent explanations to adults we'd meet in the normal course of the days ("No, I'm not excited that school starts soon because I don't go to school"). For my daughters, most of those incidents were simultaneously irritating and amusing, but both still worried that they might end up *too* different. Despite enjoying the idea that eccentric is interesting, and interesting is good, they sometimes found that appreciating their differences in the face of skeptics wore them out.

Sometimes they worried about the quality of their education. Kate spent much of her time reading and drawing. She pored over books on the history of costume and fashion, could date a garment from a painting within a decade and detect at a glance anachronisms in clothing styles in period movies. But her lack of what education bureaucrats call "a sequential, chronological course of study" concerned her at times, though never to the point that she felt called upon to do something about it. Usually, before she reached that point, she'd discover—to her amazement—when she mentioned something about Kate and Petruchio that the schooled friend she was talking with didn't know what *The Taming of the Shrew* was, or that another friend didn't know when the Civil War took place.

Other times, their problems had less to do with homeschooling itself and more to do with what happens when a parent suffers from chronic depression. When they were young, the girls often did not understand why their father was remote or moody so much of the time. As they grew older, they began to see the intractable nature of his moods, even while they were angry and resentful of them. Like many children of depressed parents, they sometimes felt responsible for his depression, believing that somehow they should be able to cheer Dad up, that if they were better daughters, he could be a more responsive father. As they've learned that they can't fix his depression for him, they've mostly grown out of their tendencies toward perfectionism.

As one who tended toward perfectionism myself when younger, I always worried about my kids being perfectionists. I'd only begun to grow out of my attempts to do everything perfectly in my late 20s, when my boss at the department store where I worked convinced me that the old saw about doing things right—"if a thing is worth doing, it's worth doing well"—is utter hogwash. The task at issue was completing that week's staff schedule, identical to the previous 50 weeks' schedules, to hand in as required to the personnel office for their files. Some things, he said, are barely worth doing adequately. It was a hard idea for me to grasp, but eventually I managed it.

That not everything needs to be done perfectly has been hard for Kate and Christie to grasp, too. We've all succeeded in internalizing the concept for tasks like housekeeping—no one really cares if we don't make perfect hospital corners with our bedsheets, nor will our house often suffer from a lack of dust bunnies or cobwebs in low crevices or high corners. Maybe it's simply an inherent part of growing up, but both girls felt at times that they needed to be high achievers according to some external, public standard.

At one point, Kate even believed—though she laughs at herself for it now—that she needed to get into a "good" college in order to prove how well homeschooling worked, that she owed it to me because of my books. Fortunately, her first-choice college rejected her application and the ensuing all-night discussion resulted in her embarking on a couple of years of community theater, after which she applied and was accepted to a theater school in New York. Once she graduated, she realized she's not cut out for life as a professional actor. She's finally begun to accept that it's okay to be what she is instead of what she thinks everybody else thinks she's supposed to be. I suspect that if she hadn't been homeschooled, that lesson would have taken the extra ten years it took me to learn.

Christie was an obstinate perfectionist. It never mattered how many times she had to try something to get it right or how hard it was—she had to make herself get it eventually. Why? I would ask, and the answer was always an emphatic "Just because." Most often, what she was getting good at was some sort of physical activity: gymnastics, kung fu, soccer, and—finally—fencing. The kid was unquestionably a visual and kinesthetic learner.

There I was, an enthusiastic reader of Alfie Kohn's *No Contest,* firmly convinced of the deleterious effects of competition. I'd grown up a reader of books, a pure spectator, an utterly sedentary creature. The one time I seriously attempted a physical activity, dance classes when Christie was a toddler, osteoarthritic knees reminded me—in no uncertain terms—that I was not an athlete.

At first, Christie didn't seem as though she was much of an athlete. Gymnastics had been fun and games. Kung fu had been more challenging, but had eventually become less interesting. Soccer was a temporary aberration, an enthusiasm prompted by the American women's World Cup championship and squelched by her placement—as a complete novice—on a team that had been playing together for three years. She finished out the season, but only out of a sense of obligation to her original commitment.

Fencing didn't seem much different. She had a great time through the six-week introductory course, but once in the regular classes, she had a terrible time keeping up with the footwork and the conditioning. For weeks, she cried in the car on the way home. "You don't have to keep doing this if you don't like it, you know," I'd say. But she insisted on continuing, even as she consistently lost bouts in both practice and competition.

Eventually, the footwork and the other conditioning had their desired effect. She developed endurance and learned the technique she needed, and gradually, over the next three or four years, Christie turned herself into a genuine athlete.

Where Kate had fenced for the pure fun of it, never caring whether she won or not (and thereby driving her coach to distraction), Christie became a serious competitor.

Fencing, like tennis and other "lifestyle" sports, is an individual sport, but a sociable one as well, which makes it well-suited to homeschoolers. Fencers compete at all ages, and while competitions are usually sorted by age, sex, and skill level, everybody can practice together. While they compete as individuals, they need each other for practice and competition, and there's a strong tradition for experienced fencers to pass their knowledge on to newer fencers, to help each other improve. As with most individual sports, beyond a basic set of skills and technique, 90% of the game is mental, learning to control nerves, to manage the stress of competition, to anticipate the opponent's moves.

Christie ate it up. She learned that practice was just that —practice. She didn't waste time and energy trying to win every touch in practice bouts, but tried out new moves and combinations until she could perform them consistently. She learned to control her frustration when she made mistakes, to let it all go and relax into the now of each touch. She learned how to want to win without wanting it too much, without letting what might be distract her from what was necessary now.

Christie's accomplished quite a bit as a fencer. She'll never make the Olympic team, but she's been nationally ranked in her age group for several years. She's earned medals at local, regional, and national competitions, and has competed in Europe. She's a nationally rated saber referee who's worked with fencers of all ages and handles angry coaches and overwrought parents with aplomb. But fencing has also taught her skills that carry over into the rest of her life. The mental skills she's developed from competition have turned out to be exactly the skills she needed to cope with her transition to college education. More than that, Christie found her passion in fencing. She's discovered she loves coaching and working with kids, and expects that, one way or another, she will be involved with fencing for the rest of her life.

I've realized, as I've watched and helped my daughters through all this, that they've become more confident as individuals as they've learned to accept less certainty in their lives. When Kate most doubted herself, she was working hardest to achieve that which the outside world would view as successful. Until she gave up striving for those extrinsic goals, she was frustrated and unable to focus. Even though she's now not sure what she might be doing next year or the year after that, she's got the self-confidence now to live with ambiguity, with the questions she doesn't yet have answers for. With Christie, it's been the certainty of her fencing knowledge that's given her the confidence that she can handle whatever else she comes to.

It's rather like what I wrote in *The Unschooling Handbook* about the consequences of kids learning to read on their own instead of with more formal instruction:

> Unschooled children seem to derive enormous confidence from learning to read this way—at their own pace, with their own methods. Reading is a skill they have developed for themselves; having mastered one of the most crucial and useful tools for future learning,

they are unlikely to believe that many subjects
or skills will be too difficult to attempt.

Year after year, we keep learning and asking questions and learning more, and time after time, we discover that it's the questions that drive us. The uncertainties, the doubts, and the ambiguities are what make our lives worth living. Having all the answers isn't nearly as interesting.

Moving Beyond the Movement

Why Homeschooling's Not Enough

Whenever I've written about homeschooling over the past twenty years, I've tried to recall what it felt like just starting out as a homeschooling parent. I wasn't one of the pioneers who had to figure out for themselves whether homeschooling was even legal or work to get laws changed in places where homeschooling actually *was* illegal. But for my first few years as a homeschooling parent, there were still plenty of questions —in the form of memos from my state's department of education, of county superintendents announcing programs to crack down on homeschoolers, of child welfare and attendance officers threatening (and occasionally conducting) truancy proceedings against homeschoolers—over whether homeschooling would continue to be a legal option for us.

Each fall we'd analyze the latest proclamations from education bureaucrats and count up the "hostile contacts" homeschoolers had with school officials. Were the auguries less ominous this year? We'd scan newspaper articles on homeschooling for evidence of public acceptance or hostility and fire off letters to the editor whenever we thought stories went too far off the deep end. We'd hold "not-back-to-school" information nights to provide accurate information to prospective homeschooling parents and create printed flyers, brochures, and pamphlets for those we couldn't reach in person.

But who exactly were "we"? We were homeschooling parents, almost—but not quite—all moms. There were usually at least once or two dads active in every homeschool organization I was ever involved with, though they were far outnumbered by the women. We were mostly in our thirties, with children ranging from infants to the early teens. Most of us were relatively new to homeschooling, thrilled to discover experienced hands who'd been at it for as long as four or five years, and completely awestruck by any veteran with seven or eight years' experience. (In retrospect, I have to feel for those few older teens we met, who must often have felt like lab animals, thoroughly—if surreptitiously—scrutinized by most of the other homeschooling parents for signs and portents of how their own children might turn out.)

Essentially, we were the homeschooling equivalent of PTA parents—the parents who, if our kids had been in school—would have been organizing fundraisers and volunteering in the classrooms. We were the next wave after those who had been personally threatened by education officials, who had received threatening letters or had to deal directly with attendance officers. Rather than working to *make* homeschooling legal, we worked to *keep* it legal, to make sure the that information and support groups were available to families who wanted to consider homeschooling as an option for their children.

We held marathon board meetings every other month, usually held at the home of a board member whose spouse and kids got to play host to the visiting kids and spouses—and occasionally dogs, too. In those five-to-eight hour meetings, we debated tactics for dealing with intransigent state bureaucrats and the best means of developing useful legislative contacts. We came up with ideas for brochures and flyers we could produce to provide information to the public, and we fought about how much we could afford to do and what our priorities should be.

Eventually, we'd adjourn to a much-anticipated—and equally marathon—potluck dinner with all the kids and spouses (and those occasional few dogs). We'd eat and talk about our kids and books we'd been reading and maybe play music and eat more, and talk some more. We'd informally review what we'd done earlier during the meeting and fantasize over all our "someday" plans.

There was a feeling among us reminiscent of one of those old Judy Garland-Mickey Rooney movies—"Let's put on a show!"—where they'd move all the livestock out of the barn and get some friends to play some music, and suddenly there was an orchestra and Busby Berkeley and sixteen costume changes. We looked for resources to help us figure out what we were doing, and we learned quite a bit through simple trial-and-error.

My own state group, the HomeSchool Association of California (still known in those days as the Northern California Homeschool Association) got lucky in its early years with the involvement of a professional graphic designer (one of our more-than-token homeschool dads) who created a whole identity package for the organization—not just a logo, but letterhead and ads and style sheets that made us look amazingly professional. This led to the peculiar experience of one of our board members, nosing around the legislature for advice on lobbying and legislation, being referred to a "really well-funded, well-organized group" that could provide guidance. When the staffer she spoke to looked up the contact information for this remarkable body that might be able to assist us, it turned out, in fact, to *be* us.

That meant we had to learn how to live up to the competent image we'd created for ourselves. One of the most important lessons we learned came from a non-profit consultant we hired to help run a board retreat to figure out our future. Typically for us, we arranged to camp out at a national recreation area, in an old army barracks that had been converted for conference use. The major differences from one of our board meetings were that there was more for the kids to do, we didn't have to cook for ourselves (though unlike many conference centers, the food was incredibly good), and the meeting went on for the whole weekend instead of the single long day we were used to.

While the kids and spouses played on the beach, we pondered the group's future. We created a mission statement and worked to develop both short-term and long-term plans, and we spent a lot of time bemoaning the fact that we had so little money that we'd never be able to do all the things we wanted to.

Diane, the non-profit consultant, would have none of it. "You're looking at things the wrong way round," she said. "Don't just sit there and tell yourselves what you can't do. You'll never do anything. Figure out what you need to do and then find a way to do it."

Figure out what we need to do and then find a way to do it? That was a concept so obvious it had never occurred to us. Could it really work?

Later that evening, a bunch of us sat around drinking wine and fantasizing about who we'd have as speakers at our ultimate homeschooling conference if we could have anybody we wanted. We settled on Micki and David Colfax, Pat Farenga or Susannah Sheffer from *Growing Without Schooling*, Grace Llewellyn (author of *The Teenage Liberation Handbook*), and John Taylor Gatto, who'd just made a splash with his book of essays, *Dumbing Us Down*. We knew we'd never get them all, but it was fun to dream, and we figured the odds of getting at least one or two of them weren't too bad.

On a rainy weekend less than three months later, we held a conference on a community college campus. Several hundred homeschooling parents and kids showed up to listen to our keynote speakers: Micki and David Colfax, Susannah Sheffer, Grace Llewellyn, John Taylor Gatto, plus—just in case they weren't enough—Peter Stillman, author of the wonderful *Families Writing*. We kept smiling all weekend, thinking, "Look what we did." We figured out what we wanted to do and we found a way to do it.

That conference also jump-started our membership growth. In barely a year, we grew from an organization of barely two hundred families to over a thousand. We thought up new things we needed to do, developing a network of county contacts, forming a serious legislative committee, upgrading our newsletter to a small magazine, making the conference an annual event, and taking the group statewide.

That was the easy part.

Becoming a larger, more active group with more members meant that more people became interested in volunteering and in running for spots on our board of directors. Those of us on the board thought this was terrific—we'd been working hard for years and were tired of always having to recruit new board members for open slots. Suddenly to have contested elections for every open position could only be a positive development, we thought.

It's an astonishingly common problem, we discovered. Tiny little non-profit organizations grow to a point where they attract new blood, and the organizational culture they've operated under during their early years is not shared by the newcomers. The old-timers are dinosaurs, unwilling to give up any of their power, say the newcomers. The newcomers don't understand how the organization works and that what they're trying to do will damage it, say the old-timers. The disapproving newcomers are obstructing the normal business of the organization, say the old-timers, while the newcomers accuse the arrogant old-timers of financial irregularities. The conflict becomes intractable—and personal—and many of those little non-profits don't survive.

HSC survived, but it was close. Our conflict cost us a board recall election, a financial audit by the state attorney general's office (we were cleared of wrongdoing), and over $10,000 in fees to an attorney who specialized in non-profit woes (and whose sliding fee scale our modest $10,000 annual budget was off the *bottom* of). Worst of all, our 80% membership renewal rate turned into a 20% renewal rate: Despite what we board members, both newcomers and old-timers believed were serious issues and principles at stake, most members viewed the conflict as mere bickering and decided to spend their dues elsewhere. It took years for HSC to recover and regain the ground lost in the conflict.

At the time of that board retreat when we hatched our growth plans and throughout the later conflict, many of us were also talking with other homeschoolers throughout the country, at first through the then-active AOL Homeschool Connection and then through other Internet venues. We shared our experiences of organizing, of dealing with government officials, of creating useful homeschooling information, and essentially tried to keep each other from having to reinvent the wheel—or struggle through the same conflict-ridden growing pains HSC had faced.

In a note at the end of his *Family Matters*, David Guterson described homeschoolers as a "contentious lot" and the politics of homeschooling as "disconcerting." At the time, many homeschooling activists were offended by those terms. I always thought they were apt, perhaps even understated. After all, there are at least three areas of homeschooling politics in which the disconcerting contentiousness reaches almost theological proportions.

Viral Learning

Most obvious, of course, is the split between the conservative, "radical right," Christian segment of the homeschooling community (what I mostly think of these days as the "Christianist" elements) and for lack of a more appropriate term, the "secular" homeschooling community, which for the purposes of this discussion encompasses both non-religious homeschoolers and those religious homeschoolers who decline to be counted among the Christianist homeschoolers. The politics at this level have been analogous to general American politics over the past few decades, with the relatively homogeneous and hierarchically organized Christianist groups often out-organizing the more diverse, laid-back secular groups, for whom their interest in keeping homeschooling legal is often their only uniting characteristic. The growth in homeschooling in the past decade, along with the often heavy-handed tactics of the Christianist groups, has reduced the influence of the Christianist camp, though the conflict certainly continues in mainstream politics.

Another area of contentious homeschool politics is the matter of homeschooler identity. To a certain extent, it seems innocuous and perfectly natural for us to think about the kind of homeschoolers we are and to publicly identify ourselves as such. For new homeschooling families who are trying to learn what their options are, it's prudent to ask around local support groups to see who's an unschooler and who takes an eclectic approach to homeschooling. If you've been reading about homeschooling styles and want to see how they work in the real world, it makes perfect sense to try to find some living examples of what you're interested in.

Most homeschoolers are eager to explain themselves and their methods to new homeschoolers—what they've tried and what's worked and why, where to find resources, and all the nitty-gritty detail of making their individual variation of their homeschooling style work for their own family. But some are adamant about declaring their homeschooling identity: "We are unschoolers" or "We are radical unschoolers." And there are a few—both individuals and entire support groups—who go beyond that to define others as well, judging whether they measure up to their own definitions of homeschooler and unschooler. (And how one reacts to such judgments depends on whether such categories are meant or interpreted as epithets.)

You might think that as someone who wrote a book called *The Unschooling Handbook*, I'd feel strongly about properly categorizing unschoolers. When I was writing the book, I strenuously urged my editors to make "unschooling" part of the book's title. At the time I wrote it, unschooling was a relatively little-known and often misunderstood approach to education, and I wanted to create a reference book that would provide useful information to those who were interested in learning more about it.

I also believed that an unschooling book from a general trade publisher might give the method a bit more mainstream respect and credibility, just as Guterson's book gave generic homeschooling a bit more credibility when it was published. It's a principle I'd discovered years earlier when my mother described the homeschooling books I'd given her to read to a librarian friend. The librarian said, "Oh, we read John Holt in one of my education classes in college." Suddenly my approach to education had considerably more credibility with my mom. If my unschooling book could help make homeschooling parents feel even a bit less nervous and self-conscious about their unconventional educational choice, I'd have provided a useful service.

But there are homeschooling parents whose purpose seems less to inspire confidence in others than to shore up their own. They proclaim, "If there is a textbook in your house, you are not an unschooler." Or, "Unschoolers don't control their children by giving them directions but allow them to learn for themselves by trial and error." (I heard once of a family like this who lost a microwave oven to their child's learning-by-doing with a few pieces of flatware.) It's a form of competitive parenting that's all too common, except that it's about homeschooling instead of SAT scores or AP classes.

Not too long ago I was interviewed for a newspaper story about unschooling. Aside from the usual questions about what unschooling is and how it works, the reporter asked me to listen to descriptions of some of the homeschooling families she had interviewed and to tell her whether or not they were unschoolers. Her descriptions were sketchy enough that I couldn't say much other than "It depends," but I balked anyway. Why on earth should I—or anybody—judge someone's homeschooling methods?

At almost every conference I speak at, there's at least one parent who fervently presses me to endorse her methods of unschooling as "right," often parsing off-hand remarks of mine or Sandra Dodd's or others to divine our "official" validation. Any homeschooler or unschooler who changes their homeschooling methods to conform to some external standard of unschooliness entirely misses the point. The point is to do whatever works best with your kids, no matter what anybody calls it. If you're making decisions about how you homeschool based on anything other than what you (and your kids) think is best for your children, you need to rethink your priorities. And anyone who tells you that you're not doing it "right" when whatever it is works for your family needs to find a new hobby.

The third area of contentious homeschooling politics, and perhaps the most contentious lately, is what I think of as the Real Homeschooler debate. It's grown out of the increasing popularity of charter schools and other public school programs designed to accommodate homeschooling families. In California, we've had such programs since at least the late '80s, originally as options for isolated families in rural counties and more recently as home study programs designed specifically to appeal to homeschoolers.

Many of us who were never interested in using such programs ourselves nonetheless favored their existence. If the state allowed and even operated homeschooling programs, it would be difficult for the state to then turn around and argue that homeschooling methods were ineffective and should be illegal. Conversely, our existence as independent homeschoolers gives the families in those programs leverage to keep those options working for them. If administrators make their program requirements too onerous, parents have the option to remove their children from the program—thereby reducing its ADA funds in proportion to the number of children who leave.

However, these programs also cause huge problems for homeschoolers. The popularity of homeschooling charter schools——offering at least partial funding along with group activities and other resources——has devastated many local support groups, drastically reducing their memberships. Support group organizers complain that charter school homeschoolers don't know state laws regarding homeschooling, that they choose activities for their children based mainly on whether they'll be reimbursed for the expense, and that they don't even try to get to know homeschoolers outside their programs.

Those local support groups aren't blameless, though. Many have what I think of as "cootie" policies, explicitly denying memberships to anyone whose children are enrolled in any kind of public school homeschooling program, on the principle that such programs are but the first step to a complete government crackdown on independent homeschooling. Sometimes the hostility seems to be simply a matter of "You're not the right kind of homeschooler, so you're not entitled to use our special term."

Phooey.

There are decent public homeschooling programs and there are terrible programs, just as there are decent private homeschooling programs and terrible ones. If public school homeschooling programs ever become a genuine threat to the right to homeschool or to the definition of what homeschooling is or isn't, it will be because independent homeschoolers and local support groups and state homeschooling organizations haven't done the work necessary to promote their own views.

If families enrolled in public programs don't know their state's laws regulating homeschooling, then state and local groups should reach out with information about the real options, not with screeds declaring homeschooling purity standards. If the public program families don't participate in local support group activities, perhaps the local groups need to re-evaluate what they have to offer those families. They may decide they are happy with the status quo or they might opt to change to accommodate a wider range of needs——each group's solutions will be different.

Some independent homeschoolers (for example, the folks behind the "We Stand for Homeschooling" petition* a few years ago) encourage homeschoolers to work to deny the vocabulary of homeschooling to any publicly funded program that seeks to attract homeschoolers, to prevent government-run programs from "co-opting" the concept of homeschooling. As a practical matter, I'm not sure how exactly that goal could be accomplished, other than writing endless letters to editors declaring that homeschoolers in public programs are not technically homeschoolers but public school students, rather like trademark lawyers fighting to keep words like "Styrofoam" or "Xerox" from becoming generic, lowercase terms.

There's a more important practical argument to be made against this eternal hostility toward public school homeschoolers: It is shortsighted and impolitic. In the long-term battle to defend homeschooling ideas and options, to maintain the freedom to choose the best form of education for our children, the people enrolled in alternative public

* See www.westandorhomeschooling.org for the complete text.

school programs are natural allies. People who choose magnet schools, charter schools, Waldorf and Montessori schools, any of the myriad non-traditional public schools are people who want flexible options for our society's kids, who believe—even though their particular version is different from ours—in having the freedom to choose whatever kind of learning works best. That their choice is different from ours does not make their potential support less valuable, and it's just plain stupid to deliberately alienate people who should be our allies.

In a way, "the homeschooling movement" is an odd thing to want to defend, rather like saying you want to defend the antiwar movement or the civil rights movement. To be a part of such a movement is to advocate a position, to promote homeschooling, to advocate civil rights, to oppose war. But to defend the movement itself? If the movement itself needs defending, maybe the movement is working itself out of its reason for existence. Perhaps we're reaching the point where homeschooling is finally perceived as a common enough option that nobody seriously questions its legitimacy any longer.

After all, haven't we all heard that modern response to the fact that we homeschool? The one when our listener says, "Oh, I'd really like to be able to do that, but I can't," almost apologizing for not homeschooling? Maybe we can be just plain homeschoolers, without needing to feel part of a uppercase Movement any longer.

But if that's the case, what are we going to do about the rest of the population, about that 90% who are stuck in NCLB schools preparing for, taking, and reviewing the results of their standardized tests? What kind of a society will our carefully raised, self-motivated learners have to live in when their colleagues and neighbors will have grown up in schools with less and less art and music and science and imagination? How will our grown homeschoolers affect that future society? And what about us, the homeschooling parents whose kids are living their own lives? What do we have to offer?

The DIY Impulse
HOME IMPROVEMENT IS ONLY THE BEGINNING

David Colfax once asked me at a conference what kind of person I was. "Are you an optimist or a pessimist?" After a little reflection, I told him, only half-seriously "I think of myself as a cynical optimist." Since then, I've decided my oxymoronic quip was a fairly accurate description of how I view the world.

Being a cynic is pretty easy these days, what with our appallingly misguided foreign ventures, threatened civil rights, corporate malfeasance and income inequality amounting to a second Gilded Age, foodstuffs contamination, famine, genocide, global warming and other environmental hazards—the catastrophic list goes on and on. It's not just the big stuff, either—there is plenty to discourage at smaller scales, too: real estate scams, steroid abuse in sports, academic cheating, Nigerian princes seeking to share misplaced fortunes, media fascination with celebrity misbehavior, credulous belief in baseless cancer cures and "male enhancement products."

It's impossible to read a newspaper without discovering yet another example of self-serving behavior, yet another disaster to add to the accumulation of horrors. The cynic in me is no longer surprised at each new revelation, each confirmation of the idea that's it's best simply to expect the worst.

And yet . . .

And yet I am still shocked. Shocked at each and every instance of behavior that—in that phrase from the Geneva Conventions that we shouldn't need to be so familiar with—"shocks the conscience." Despite all the revelations, despite being completely unsurprised by the abhorrent acts humans are not only capable of but do perpetrate, I am still shocked by it all.

That's the optimist in me, the part that expects decent and humane behavior from most people most of the time. The optimistic part of me may sometimes be demoralized by events, but is never crushed into indifference or despair. By some quirk of fate or temperament or genetics, I am incorrigibly hopeful, even when expecting the worst is the only sane response to current events.

It's a characteristic that often drives my daughters nuts. They call me a Pollyanna, unrealistic and deluded. They accuse me of feigning hope and cheer as some weird variant of a self-esteem program, just to keep them from being discouraged or depressed. But it's not sham or pretense—it's genuine: I am a congenitally hopeful individual.

Lately, though, I've begun to notice a few traces of evidence for my chronic buoyancy, items here and there from my "duh research," in political news, within the homeschooling community, and on the Internet. Everywhere I look, I keep seeing signs of the same trends.

Preparing to speak at a homeschooling conference recently, I reviewed one of the talks I planned to give, one I've done for years, "The Hidden Hazards of Homeschooling." It's mainly an affectionate collection of recognizable homeschooler quirks—our messy houses, our overflowing bookshelves, our tendency to collect and hoard astonishing amounts of "stuff" (some might even call it "junk") on the off-chance we or our kids might find it useful one day—but there's a serious theme, too. One of the major homeschooling hazards I cite is that in raising our kids to be independent thinkers who aren't afraid to question authority, our kids often become independent thinkers who aren't afraid to question authority—and sometimes the authorities they question are their parents.

Not only that, but most of the time, the process is contagious and infectious. Perhaps it's only that in modeling the behavior we'd like to see our kids adopt, we reinforce our own penchant for independent thinking beyond what we already possessed, but inevitably we learn just as much from the homeschooling process as they do. That's where the idea of "viral learning" comes from—we can't immunize ourselves from the consequences of the educational choices we've made for our kids.

What I've realized since my daughters left home is that we have not just launched our kids out into the world. We homeschooling parents have launched ourselves out there, too. It's not just this younger, upcoming generation we've got to watch to see what they can do——it's us, too.

Most of the veteran moms who answered my questionnaire for this book didn't just run out and join the workforce as soon as their kids left home. More often, they've pieced together an ever-changing patchwork of part-time work, volunteerism, and self-employment. It's a pattern described by a speaker I met at a homeschool conference in Virginia a few years back. In *Free Agent Nation*, Daniel Pink contends that a 10%-and-growing segment of the American population is doing the same thing. Not a homeschooling parent himself (though he said it was definitely something he'd consider when he had kids), he was intrigued by the number of homeschooling families who seemed to be on the leading edge of what he sees as a major trend. More and more workers, he says, are less and less willing to work at mind-numbing jobs with fewer and fewer benefits and not all that much job security. More and more prefer to find something they love doing, something that makes what feels like a positive contribution to society or to the world, even if it means less income.

Then I came across the idea of emergent systems. What's an emergent system? Think ant colonies or slime molds—— populations of individuals all milling around aimlessly until suddenly enough of them are heading in the same direction to coalesce into a purposeful organism. Or consider the software that lets merchants like Amazon recommend books that might interest you based on the other books that people who bought the same book you did bought. There's not an ant general or a head slime mold cell or a single reader who suddenly gives an order that the larger group obeys. It's the actions of all the individual components of the group that create a critical mass that transforms the group from a random crowd into something that looks like it's acting intentionally.

The concept is also the basis for recent theories of how our minds work, how individual neurons create intelligence. It appears that our brains work similarly to the ants and the slime mold cells, with neurons appearing to fire randomly until enough activate along the same pathways to create a perception or a thought. Emergence is about how individual bits working independently can create a whole qualitatively different from those parts, how "brain" can become "mind."

The Internet teems with emergent systems. Wikipedia is a prime example of a project that would be both unimaginable and unmanageable if it operated in top-down fashion. As of late July 2007, Wikipedia contained nearly 8 million articles in over 250 languages, with nearly 2 million articles in the English language version.* Frequently criticized for its reliance on volunteer authors and relatively open editing access, by which nearly anyone can add or alter articles, it far outstrips conventional encyclopedias in scope and timeliness. It's notable also for its insistence on documentation rather than expertise. Unlike most conventional encyclopedias, which

---

* http://en.wikipedia.org/wiki/Wikipedia, of course.

solicit recognized academic experts to write articles, Wikipedia doesn't care who writes its articles as long as the facts within them are documented. Further, the several hundred volunteer editors note the reliability and biases of articles as well as repair damage caused by the occasional vandals. The result is a valuable general reference that is among the top ten most-visited websites in the world, quite a remarkable feat for an enterprise with no editor-in-chief.

Wikipedia is just the beginning. The fastest growing segments of the Internet are the viral, bottom-up, emergent sites. Social networking sites, even though commercial operations, have mushroomed through the actions of their users linking to each other in ever more complex webs of contacts.

And then there are YouTube and the blogs, which have begun to revolutionize American politics. Howard Dean's presidential campaign used blogs and email to mobilize volunteers and donors all over the country. Since then, dozens of progressive Congressional candidates have built support by posting their campaign ads not just on their own websites but also on YouTube——far less expensive than television and radio advertising——and participating on the major progressive political blogs like DailyKos, Firedoglake, TPMmuckraker, and Digby, inviting participation in their campaigns. This kind of campaigning is not "push" campaigning, where ads and statements are pushed at passive viewers through one-way media like television. It's a "pull" process, where the content has to be substantial enough and appealing enough to get people talking about it and linking to it and showing it to their friends and colleagues. It transforms "viewers" into participants and actors.

Many of the political blogs are beginning to blur the lines between blogs and news media, with bloggers like The Next Hurrah's Marcy Wheeler and Firedoglake's Jane Hamsher and Christy Hardin Smith "liveblogging" Congressional hearings and events such as the Libby trial, providing more detailed reports than the traditional print and broadcast news media.

During the investigations into the U.S. Attorney firings when the Justice Department released emails on late Friday afternoons in hopes that the documents would escape notice over the weekend, blogs such as TPMmuckraker linked to copies posted online and asked for volunteers to help read them all and post comments on any interesting bits they found. Combing through a mass of data like that is an almost impossible task for a single conventional news organization to accomplish, particularly when at least partly motivated by the desire to scoop competitors. But random interested volunteers online—both lawyers and lay people—can read and analyze huge volumes of material and publicly discuss their findings within a matter of hours. And those findings are available to the public, to the press, to investigators, and to lawmakers to use immediately. Instead of disappearing into a weekend news void, Friday night document dumps become objects of citizen scavenger hunts, with interesting finds trumpeted on multiple blogs and passed on to mainstream news media. That's something new in our political process.

YouTube has had similar viral effects—it's not just the entertaining videos like the Diet Coke and Mentos fountains or piano-playing cats that have users flocking to the site.

Political gaffes like Virginia's (now former) Senator George Allen's "macaca" moment don't just disappear after a day or two in the news—they are played and linked to and relinked to the point that they can influence election results.

In short, the Internet and its assorted viral systems have made communications accessible to the general population. It's not radio or television, which are one-way communication formats (we give you the program, you watch and listen). It's not even a two-way format like the telephone, where one person can talk to another. It's a many-to-many medium, unlike anything that's existed before, but one that offers enormous possibilities for citizen participation.

I used to be impressed with how easy email made it for homeschool activists across the country to communicate with each other, offering ideas and support to each other. But what we did is negligible compared to some of the projects being created today by people who've never met, who know each other only by relatively anonymous screen names. For example, one of the best collections of energy policy proposals floating around for consideration these days is not from a think tank or a foundation or a lobbying firm, but from a group of DailyKos contributors—working citizens who've developed concrete proposals for achieving energy independence for the United States by 2040.* If that's not cause for optimism, I don't know what would be.

One of the questions I ask in that "Homeschooling Hazards" talk is a play on one that homeschooling critics sometimes ask, intending it to highlight what a silly idea homeschooling must be: What if everybody did it? My answer

* http://www.ea2020.org/drupal/node

always begins by asking the question back: What *if* everybody did it? Wouldn't it be interesting if more and more people homeschooled, if more and more of us took control of greater portions of our lives? How will our crop of independent thinkers acting to change the world *actually* change the world?

I was always speaking theoretically, of some future time when we could look back and see ourselves having made incremental changes in how we lived. I was looking at how we homeschoolers created and grew our movement. I was speculating about what could be, and it turns out that while I was speculating, the world was already changing.

We——as homeschoolers——are a part of this new emerging grassroots world, but we are only a tiny part. Daniel Pink may have been right in that talk back in Virginia that we were on the leading edge of a trend, but the trend reaches far beyond our single-little issue.

When I was a kid, I used to wish sometimes that I lived in a more exciting time, such as during the American Revolution, when that collection of Enlightenment gentlemen created a document with one of the best opening lines ever written:

> We the people of the United States, in order to form a more perfect union, establish justice, insure domestic tranquility, provide for the common defense, promote the general welfare, and secure the blessings of liberty to ourselves and our posterity, do ordain and establish this Constitution for the United States of America.

I've always loved the Preamble to the Constitution, both its cadence and its content. It's a concise and precise statement of the purpose of our government, and it makes it unmistakably, indisputably clear from whose authority that government is established.

We the people.

It's not an abstract concept. Nor is it just some phrase we get to memorize in eighth grade (or whenever homeschoolers get around to learning about government). It's the incarnation of Jefferson's "yeomen farmers"—the citizens who would and should be active participants in making and maintaining our society. Not many of us are farmers any longer, but we're still the building blocks, the individuals from whom the greater purpose emerges.

I've decided I don't need any other time to live in—our current times are interesting enough.

We've been lost for a hundred years or so, as we grew so large and so quickly that we lost our means of talking with each other and let big business and corporations and one-way media do the talking for us. But we're finding our way back again, finally, bit by bit learning for ourselves, learning to do for ourselves. We're learning to believe in ourselves again, learning to be optimistic about our power and our future, learning to be what we should be:

WE THE PEOPLE

Appendix

When I first started working on this book, I created another long questionnaire to inflict on my homeschooling friends and acquaintances, just as I did for *The Homeschooling Handbook* and *The Unschooling Handbook*. My questionnaires are never easy little collections of multiple-choice questions like marketing surveys. There are always a few short-answer items for general background information, but since I don't even pretend to attempt a scientific survey, the bulk of the questions are essentially open-ended essay prompts.

I tried answering one of my questionnaires once, but it was more than I could make myself finish, so I've always been astounded and indebted to everyone who sent me responses. Many of my respondents have told me it took them several days or even a couple of weeks to finish, but that they enjoyed the opportunity to think seriously about their approaches to homeschooling and parenting. A few have helped with every book I've written, for which I am particularly grateful.

When I created the questionnaire for *Viral Learning*, I intended to use the responses in the same way I used those for my first two books. But as I thought more about what I wanted to write and as I began to receive completed questionnaires, I realized that the responses wouldn't fit into the text the same way the earlier responses had worked in the earlier books.

But much of what I received was wonderful stuff to read. When I finished collating everything so that I could read all the answers to each question together, the aggregate effect was something I couldn't bear to leave out of the book entirely.

Hence, this appendix, which I think of as a virtual group hug—encouraging and knowledgeable stories and advice from homeschoolers who've homeschooled for a cumulative total of (approximately) 250 years with more than 35 kids. (I considered trying to calculate actual child-years of homeschooling, but it got too complicated, what with some kids trying school and then leaving again, and some starting homeschooling after having been in school.)

Q: *When and why did your family begin homeschooling?*

I started looking at every school around and finally came to the conclusion that if we wanted an individualized program, we'd have to create our own. I suddenly realized we could homeschool very happily. At the time, there was a little homeschool program offered by a local public school, and in those early days, unlike now, those programs were very non-intrusive and supportive. It worked out fine for a while, although it only took a few meetings with them to realize that they actually had no particular guidance to offer us that we couldn't figure out better on our own.—*Lillian Jones, CA*

When Candra was one year old, I quit my job as clinical coordinator of a university and went to work for a special education cooperative serving four counties in the public schools. My experiences there confirmed that school simply was not a healthy way for children to grow up, particularly any kind of square-peg child who didn't fit the round holes, as many of the kids I saw for services were.

When Calen was five, I asked him, "So, are you at all interested in trying school?" He responded with a vehement "No!" I asked, "Why not?" and he replied, "Because I want to be just Calen!"— *Leslie McColgin, KY*

When Zachary was five years old and very securely attached to me, I could see no reason to send him away for hours every day. He was a bright vivacious kid and he'd got that way on his own at home with me. I thought, what's so magical about the age of five that suddenly life has to change so drastically?—*Christine Sanders, IA*

It always puzzled me why school had to make interesting things so dull in order to teach them. Historical movies were fascinating. History texts were sleep-inducingly dull. *Nova* was fascinating but all the interesting stuff got sucked out before it was put in the science textbook. Watching *Oedipus* and *Pride and Prejudice* teleplays was riveting. Being made to read *Silas Marner* was tedious.

It became obvious that unless my daughter thought the lessons were fascinating, it would come to a point where I'd be making her do something she didn't want to do, which would be no better than school. I worked my way through unit studies and eclectic. All of them ultimately came down to the same thing: I had to hope she wanted to do the activities or I'd have to make her. The most commonly asked questions [in online homeschooling forums] were "What's the best program?" and "What do you do when they won't do their lessons?" The only group that focused on learning being fun were the unschoolers. I read what they wrote because I liked the attitude of respect they had for kids and the outlook that life was learning and learning was fun. They were way too unconcerned about academics for my taste but eventually I caught on to what unschooling was all about and realized that it wasn't an unconcern for academics but an entirely different approach to learning.—*Joyce Fetteroll, MA*

Knowing my child now, [homeschooling] was the right decision. She would never do well in a school setting. She thinks too differently and too fast. She wants to know the answers to the questions in her head now—not when the curriculum says it's time to talk about it. She is a whole-to-parts learner and repetition makes her crazy.—*Samantha Fenner, NH*

Q: What approach (school-at-home/eclectic/unschooling/any variants thereof) did your family start with? If you've got more than one child, how different or similar was the process for each? How did the process change over the years? Were changes consistently in one direction (structured to relaxed or vice versa) or varied according to need?

I wanted to be structured. I wanted cute desks with their names in stencils and neat piles of well-loved books. I love the smell of new books and the moment when you open a new workbook. [My kids] taught me that they had to be approached with things that are useful and from the perspective of their current interest.—*Shannon Anderson, MN*

We started with a very relaxed, eclectic approach. I had Conor write in his journal each night. We did math games and science experiments and I read to him a lot. I was trying to make everything an educational experience. I used a lot of school methods at first because it was the only thing I knew. This only lasted for a few months. It all felt so false. I started feeling like I was pulling him away from doing things he loved and was actively engaged in to make him do things that I thought would foster learning. Many times it frustrated him and many times it made us both unhappy. I didn't see how this would benefit his learning. So I read more and moved toward an unschooling approach which quickly evolved into full-on radical unschooling.—*Mary Gold, OR*

I did creative little lessons of my own design with him, but soon gave up the notion of "teaching" him because I kept seeing him learning in amazing ways about any number of things, and I could see being "taught" was more of a hindrance than a help. I don't think I ever thought to label what we did—people didn't tend to do that so much in those days.

It's not as if I didn't have periodic anxiety attacks right up to the end, but there was mostly an underlying understanding, from observing the way he learned, that everything was going to work out fine. I was nonetheless surprised when he started classes at the local community college in his teens and didn't need any remedial tips on his writing skills.—*Lillian Jones, CA*

I've noticed myself learning right alongside the kids, not teaching in the traditional sense. I see the same phenomenon in many homeschooling families. We begin discovering together rather than imparting our knowledge. I wish we could lose the negative pictures that unschooling brings up. I preferred the term "child-led learning" for a long time. It seemed like a better description of what we were doing. Now I don't think too much about what we are doing, we just do it. It's like describing to someone how you breathe or encourage their heart to beat. We just live and learn—that simple.—*Leslie Buchanan, CA*

When my third child came along, I was already thoroughly disillusioned with school. First, I had my own less-than-stellar history to reflect on, then the years of coping with the system on behalf of my first two kids. when this girl proved to be both precocious and also the most stubborn individual I've ever met, I know she would never be happy at school.

My two very different girls have taught me well how to leave them alone to educate themselves. Where, from my experience with Virginia, I had the idea that reading was easily accomplished through predictable steps, Olivia showed me that was not a universal process. She refused point-blank to have anything to do with alphabet books. She never wanted to discuss letter sounds at all. If I invited her to partake in such an activity she'd put me off with "maybe later." She never wanted to learn the alphabet or how to count to ten. Somehow she did learn those things, but I can testify that she did not learn them from me. What she did was write. At four, she'd station herself wherever I was and ask me to spell words for her for what seemed like hours on end. Frequently she'd have to interrupt herself to ask how to form a letter, but she'd be transcribing my spellings the whole time. At the end of the process there'd be a paragraph that I could read back to her, but she couldn't read it herself.

At eight, she still wasn't reading, which I know because she was in a choir and couldn't follow the lyrics at Christmas time. That spring she latched onto the Reader Rabbit software program, which she did from start to finish each time, in marathon sittings. Soon after, she announced she could read *The Runaway Bunny* and only a few weeks later was arguing with her sister about borrowing her 9–

12 level fiction book. At no juncture was I welcomed into the process, except to hear her read on occasion. This was my postgraduate work in unschooling, I think. It went against the grain for me, but she was very clear that it was her business, not mine.

I moved from relaxed to practically comatose in my approach over the years. I still suggest things I think will fit with the direction the girls are taking, and I am now trying to guide Virginia a bit in learning math because she is interested in qualifying for a high school diploma, and I am really clear it's not my decision.—
Maureen Berger, BC

I had been heavily influenced by my language development background as a speech language pathologist. The late '70s and early '80s saw a tremendous paradigm shift in how children with language difficulties were treated, and what was called "pragmatics" became very important. So therapy for children began using more "natural" contexts and started emphasizing things like "child-initiated" activity, the child choosing and controlling the topics and the functions of language. Just having a child name pictures or toys presented by a therapist, even in play, was no longer considered appropriate. Language needed to be for the purpose of accomplishing many various real social-communicative functions— kids use language to express notice, request information (learn about the world), interact socially, express feelings, request objects and actions, and yes, sometimes to simply name items or give information to others.

An example in our homeschooling was very clear to me the year Candra would have been in kindergarten. We had a neighbor boy the same age and his mother was bemoaning his resistance to being told what to do at school. He had stayed up until 2:00 a.m. arguing that he wasn't going to do his homework for kindergarten, which involved writing his name for six pages (I think about 50 times). Shortly after this, my daughter mentioned that she thought she ought to put her name in all her little picture books she loved so well, like *Strega Nona* and *Amelia Bedelia*. So she sat down and wrote her name in probably far more than 50 books. That's pragmatics.

So from the very beginning I had a strong sense that any activity was to be meaningful and purposeful from the child's point of view—never just to please an adult who had decided it was something the child "should" know or do. And I could see that if language was learned best when it was child-initiated, other areas of learning could be also.

Psychologist Jerome Bruner has proposed that there are two main modes of understanding the world: the narrative and the logical. My kids seem to represent extremes in these, for some unknown reason, as my husband and I are apparently more blends of the two. Candra is my narrative child, with words and stories pouring out of her from an early age—she was creating poetry by age three, and creating stories for her friends all the time. Calen is extremely logical and has always been drawn to mechanical and logical activities, with no interest in stories at all. He does watch an occasional movie, but that's about it. Emotionally, Candra has always been up and down and all over the place with extreme variations, while Calen is steady and in the middle, never overly enthusiastic or terribly upset.

One of my favorite memories is the year we got a camcorder for the family at Christmas. The kids were excited about the new "toy" and started concocting plans for what they could do with it. On their own, they decided to put on a "newscast," with Calen doing the tech work and Candra the announcing. They worked on it for maybe a week or so, mostly when I was off working, and then put on the show for us. At one point during the show, Candra has Calen zoom in on a picture of Queen Elizabeth I in a book, and she says, "And now, for a brief moment in history . . . " The camera goes back to her and she stares straight at the camera and talks for maybe 10 or 15 minutes about Queen Elizabeth. Afterward, I asked her if Calen was holding up note cards or something—how could she talk that long without notes? "Oh, mom! I love Queen Elizabeth and I know all kinds of things about her. I could probably talk for 30 minutes!"—*Leslie McColgin, KY*

I remember despairing that I could never document all of the interesting conversations that we had, the two- to five-minute conversations that made up most of our days, the contents of which added together created a coherent understanding of the world.—*Carol Burris, FL*

Q: What were the most difficult aspects of homeschooling? What were the most fun or interesting parts?

The most difficult aspect of homeschooling has been the entrance of the Evangelical crowd and the backlash. The Evangelicals thought I was homeschooling "wrong" and the people who entered from the secular side regularly confused me with the Evangelicals.—*Julia Biales, NY*

The experts are the most difficult part. I've learned that anyone telling me about their pet ideology is going to trip me up. Anyone who has all of the answers will meet my children and change their mind. I've even had a social worker who was supposed to be an advocate for Niki go from horrified "How can you homeschool an autistic child?" to "Can I have this mother contact you?" and work with me to start a respite program in the county.

It's also the housework part. Where you live is supposed to be this grand sweep of beautiful color and unused furniture with delicate vases of freshly cut flowers. This isn't realistic in a house where children actually live. A real home is books all over, easy blanket access, pens and pencils on every surface. A real home has a place for the lava lamp, glue sticks, Post-Its, three kinds of paint, clay, and more books than you thought one human could own. That conflict between what's expected of a "housekeeper" versus what a mother actually does can be very difficult to prioritize.— *Shannon Anderson, MN*

When I was growing up, the most difficult part was always feeling different from everyone around you. They'd talk about things you had no idea about, like the different teachers at the local school or the last school dance or football game. They wouldn't mean to, but I'd be excluded from those conversations. I wasn't particularly interested in those things, and I didn't mind not knowing about them, but it could be lonely.—*Myranda Brown, SC*

The most fun parts definitely involved learning together. It was fun watching the grass snake weave its way through the chain link fence. It was fun learning to draw together, comparing our finished products. It was fun playing Rummy Roots and expanding our vocabularies and playing with words.

I've had a hard time forgiving myself for pushing Thomas into math phobia. I don't know how many times, even in the last few years of homeschooling, I had to go running to another homeschooling parent for reassurance that I was not a lousy homeschool mother. Self-doubt is dangerous stuff; it can tear down a homeschooling mother quicker than just about anything else.— *Tammy Cardwell, TX*

Difficult? It would have been having to coordinate with other parents in smoothly maintaining the support group community. You don't necessarily have a lot more in common than the fact that you homeschool, but it's important to keep things happening and to have some sort of ongoing homeschooling community for social life and activities. That became especially true in the teen years. It sometimes seemed like a drain to be going off to this and that group or activity, but I think it all balanced out. And it took effort to keep the social activities ongoing—relationships and friendships need to be sought out and nurtured.—*Lillian Jones, CA*

Just being with the kids all the time, hearing every squabble, it took a lot of practice for me not to step in and referee each time. Part of life is learning to deal with conflict, so I realized that the kids had to be able to communicate with each other without me. Still, the housework staring you in the face and the kids picking at each other can be the catalyst for an impromptu field trip or park day, or even just a trip to the market.

What I love most is having the kids all to myself (the same thing that can make it hard). No one dictates our days to us. No one gives us deadlines or assignments to complete. We can change our minds at the last minute about what we've planned for the day. If we are sick or tired we can take a day off and lie around. We can bake, read, hike, play. Our lives belong to us. Now that the oldest, Damon, has gone off to school (his choice—football), I really appreciate the freedom we still have at home.—*Leslie Buchanan, CA*

I love that we are so close—and even the girls' dad and I still share that experience. The girls may fight with each other but still are infinitely closer than I was with my siblings. Of course, there is the dark side of that interdependence—certain brief moments of the last ten years saw me wishing I could ship them both somewhere far away from me.

There has been a repeated phenomenon over the years: often when I start to feel anxious because some skill or area of knowledge might be missed, one of the girls will suddenly demonstrate mastery of that very thing soon afterward. Maybe I'm sensing their readiness for that, without realizing they are, too?

Viral Learning

I love that my girls take for granted that I'll be interested in what they are doing. This, I observe, is not the case for everyone with teenagers.—*Maureen Berger, BC*

Sometimes other kids said things that made my kids worry a bit. It was easily refuted, and in retrospect now they see that in every case those kids are less content and less "successful" (at this point in time) than they are. This might not remain true, as maybe fifteen years out, "success" will look like master's degrees and such for some of them, but we don't know that our kids won't move in that direction, too. If they do, it will be from choice and joy, not from "it's time to go to college; just go; you're going."

That leapfrog effect is seen in many aspects of life. When they were eight, they felt behind. When they were 13, they felt ahead; when they were 16 they felt behind. When they're 18, they feel ahead. So if at 30 they feel behind, I wouldn't be at all surprised if at 40, they feel ahead again, as others become disillusioned with careers they chose too soon, for reasons of prestige or income.

All cases will vary, I'm sure, and change as the years pass, but the fears they had when other seven-year-olds assured them they would never have jobs when they grew up, or would never learn to read, are distant and amusing memories.—*Sandra Dodd, NM*

The most difficult aspect of homeschooling for me in the early years was what I sensed as disapproval from my parents. Although we knew the kids would not be returning to school, we claimed that it was a year-by-year decision as a way to minimize their spoken and unspoken doubts.—*Carol Burris, FL*

Learning to have patience with myself has been the most difficult aspect—patience that it will click, that we can stop to smell the roses, that we can read that piece again next year.

Most interesting: learning all the things I should have learned years ago. So many things make so much more sense now! It has been surprising to find the things I somehow just completely missed. Some of that may have been due to moves my family made, school changes, and some, I'm sure, to just zoning out. But I was always an honor student, top five per cent of my class. How did I pull that off without having any more basic knowledge than this? That, and the career and skill changes my husband and I have gone through during our working lives, have made firm my belief that knowing how to learn is a vital skill, probably more important to one's happiness through life than waving a diploma or degree around.—*Jo Craddock, LA*

Q: Is there anything you wish you'd done (or not done) from the beginning?

I wish I had had more confidence in my ability in the beginning to rise to the challenge—but discovering what I had inside me was part of the process for me.

I wish I had learned to say "yes" earlier in the process. In the early years I was more bound by the first reaction to a suggestion from the kids. As the years went by I learned to brainstorm more and find new or different ways to get to a similar result. Instead of saying "No, we can't do that because . . .," I learned to say "Well, let's see if there's a way to do that."—*Carol Burris, Fl*

Q: What advice would you give to the then-you based on what you know now?

I'd tell myself never to read books that told parents what kids "should" be doing at a particular age.—*Maureen Berger, BC*

Q: How did your kids turn out? Do you like them? How much influence do you think having homeschooled had on who they are and what they do?

I think I turned out fine. My friends say I'm weird, but I happen to like weird. I don't blindly follow society. I have my own business, instead of working for someone else. I research things instead of just believing what the "experts" say. I think homeschooling made me a stronger person. I'm seeing that it's making my kids stronger in themselves. They don't hesitate to tell a friend or stranger "no"; they don't blindly go along with the crowd. They aren't embarrassed to share their thoughts or beliefs.

I hope they don't ever lose that confidence.—*Myranda Brown, SC*

Homeschooling made all the difference, not because it changed who they are, but because it let them be free from the peer pressure to disguise who they are. They've been very choosey about who they spend time with, based on who appreciates them and has something to offer that they appreciate in turn. I think they respect differences and value uniqueness in a way that most schooled teens unfortunately don't. I think growing up surrounded by people who truly cared about them, appreciated and loved them, gave them an advantage.—*Maureen Berger, BC*

I like them, they amuse me, they inspire me, and we're friends. They trust me and confide in me and ask my advice. I ask their advice.—*Sandra Dodd, NM*

She loves to learn. When she was eight, she was asked if she got the summer off from school. She didn't understand the question. "You know, so you don't have to learn stuff all summer long." She was shocked. "Why would I want to stop doing something as fun as learning for a whole summer? Don't you think learning is fun?" The man nearly spit his coffee out at her.—*Samantha Fenner, NH*

Q: How did your homeschooling affect the person you are now? Do you think it has made you a different person than you might otherwise have been?

I'm a much stronger person than when I started out. I believed in the educational caste thing. The doctor knows best, the teacher knows best. After many, many, *many* incidents, I'm convinced that the experts are merely justifying their college loans. A real person can stand up and *be* anything. You can go into city council meetings, you can stand up before the school board, you can put on the appropriate costume and be anything from super-professional to purple clown.—*Shannon Anderson, MN*

I am more outspoken than I would have been, more willing to take a stand on issues and speak out than I might have been without the education I got while guiding my children. Too, though the people around me laugh when I say it, I was always horrendously shy. Getting involved in the homeschool world and sharing with other moms and dads who needed what my experience could give them brought me out of a pretty thick shell. —*Tammy Cardwell, TX*

Homeschooling provided a lot of things to think about, stimulated a lot of activities and travel I might not have thought to pursue, and keeps me busy thinking to this day about all this. Thinking about one's own experience with homeschooling can't help but lead to thought about learning and education as a whole— and about what's happening in the education world. I still put a lot of time into helping newcomers to homeschooling, because I realize what an effect a happy homeschooling experience can have on the lives of a child and a family.—*Lillian Jones, CA*

I've grown a lot along with my kids. I have worked through parenting issues that I inherited from my upbringing. I've learned to have the courage of my convictions and depart from "what everybody knows." I've become more patient and maybe just a touch more tactful (but it's still not my strong suit).—*Maureen Berger, BC*

I see learning in a very different way than I did 14 years ago, which makes me see society's beliefs about what is necessary for "success" in a different light. It's difficult to see parents struggling with what they feel they need to do to give their kids the foundation for success as adults when I know it's not necessary.—*Joyce Fetteroll, MA*

Homeschooling has made me more patient. It has also made me more likely to go after something I want to learn or do, keeping the idea of lifelong learning an active state, rather than just curling up with a book. Right now I am taking a quilting class after years of wanting to learn to quilt. I am also actively preparing to teach some classes related to some of my passions—writing and crafts. I'm not sure I would have been willing to move that far out of my comfort zone without the years of homeschooling behind me.—*Carol Burris, FL*

I am much more likely to open my mouth about something. I no longer want to be invisible. I enjoy learning new things again.—*Samantha Fenner, NH*

Q: If your kids are now grown and moved out, have you had a hard time adjusting? How serious was any "empty nest" syndrome?

It was a lot harder for me than for some parents I've seen who hadn't spent so much time with their kids over the years. I find their detachment kind of odd, as a matter of fact. It's never occurred to me not to keep active and carry on with my own life, though. I went back to some of the things I'd dropped along the way—like painting—and found I could get just as excited about them as ever and still enjoy learning more about them.—*Lillian Jones, CA*

Q: How are your relationships with your kids different from what they were when they were younger? Do you see those relationships as different from those of families you know who did not homeschool for any length of time?

I am amazed at how easy it has been to transition from being completely responsible for their welfare to allowing them more and more freedom and discretion.—*Maureen Berger, BC*

I see kids being less open with their parents than my daughter is. There is a distance between them when kids are aware that what they reveal could mean disapproval or loss of privileges. Even a schooled friend of my daughter's who has a good relationship with her parents can get sarcastic with them, often because they are living separate lives from each other.—*Joyce Fetteroll, MA*

In my experience, relationships like those I have with my children are much harder to find among parents who did not homeschool. Not impossible, but far rarer. I think the experience of living our lives by spending most of our time together provides a basic grounding within a family which is more difficult to achieve when your days are spent apart.

The difference is not simply one that grows out of an educational choice. Rather, it grows out of a fundamentally different view of children. When children are expected to behave in developmentally appropriate ways, their needs are met, and they are treated as individuals deserving of respect regardless of their age, they can spread their wings and soar, viewing the world as a place of comfort and beauty. A sense of place, purpose, and well-being pervades their relationships. When children are more rigidly controlled and corrected, expected to fit into someone else's mold and not allowed the time to be children, the world becomes a less secure and welcoming place.—*Carol Burris, FL*

There's that oft-repeated statement I think all homeschoolers have heard from non-homeschoolers: "I couldn't take being around my kids that much." I enjoy being around my kids. it's not all roses —we all know each other's buttons intimately—but I think a big part of learning at home is that they (and we) learn how to be better roommates, office mates, and world mates—roles we will have as long as we're on this earth.—*Jo Craddock, LA*

Q: Do you consider yourself a feminist? Has that changed since or because of having homeschooled? Has being a feminist conflicted with your homeschooling views? Have you worried about how your children would learn to view gender roles because you were a "non-working" parent?

I'm a working parent—always have been—and so was my mother. Yes, we're all feminists, going back to my grandmother, who was a suffragist.

Nothing I have ever encountered in the most extreme exclusive religious circles has come even into the same category as the hostility that feminist circles have dished out.

There isn't one feminism, just like there isn't one homeschooling.—*Julia Biales, NY*

Homeschooling means that someone needs to be with the kids to guide, enrich, and learn with them. I don't think my children have stereotyped a woman's role just because we decided that I was the best one to stay home with them. Even though I was the one at home, our household duties were always mixed up and shared. Jon did most of the cooking and helped with laundry while I mowed the lawn and painted the bedrooms. Life is a shared experience. My children understand that.—*Mary Gold, OR*

I am a feminist from way back. If there has been any effect of attachment parenting and homeschooling, it has been to point up the need to reaffirm the woman's right to choose her lifestyle. Then, also, there should be an acknowledgment that families have to adapt to reality. I think feminists must get real about the needs of small children, to recognize that what's good for them is a consistent, loving caretaker—father, mother, or other—but someone with a stake in the child, not just a paycheck.—*Maureen Berger, BC*

The world is changing, and it's hard to know how many women—or men—will even be able to make the choice to stay home in the future.—*Lillian Jones, CA*

I consider myself a feminist but expanded that to consideration of the societal assumptions that need to change to give the same opportunities to both sexes. We decided for practical reasons— health insurance being a major factor—that my husband would be the outside worker. If universal health care had been available, would we have made the same choice? At least we might have had a choice! A homemaker, either sex, needs health care coverage and retirement funding. I've been a working parent throughout their lives, and the kids have been made keenly aware of the choices available (or not). I think they've learned that marriage and family life are not 50/50. A commitment to another person or persons means that sometimes it might be 50/50, but it's more often 20/80 or 75/25, or sometimes even 100/0.—*Jo Craddock, LA*

Q: Have you found that others have made assumptions about you or your views because your family homeschooled?

I get really, really exasperated at the people who assume that we're hard-core creationists who are protecting our children from secular humanism. I've only met about three families who fit the homeschool stereotype as it's portrayed in the media. I'm not locking them in the basement. I'm not avoiding real issues, and I'm certainly not keeping them from society.—*Shannon Anderson, MN*

In the early years of our homeschooling, when it wasn't so well-known, people often made the assumption that we were a Christian fundamentalist family. I went out of my way to let it be known that we homeschooled to bring more of the world into our children's lives rather than to shelter and keep things from them.—*Mary Gold, OR*

The only assumptions I have encountered relate to how we homeschool. People now assume we use a charter school and "school at home." They also seem to assume that my kids are academically advanced.—*Leslie Buchanan, CA*

Mostly I meet people who have a total misconception about how arduous homeschooling is, what a sacrifice I'm making, and some assume that I must have a teaching certificate. Then there are the ones who ask, "Oh, do you homeschool them yourself, or do you have people who come to your house to do that?" Which puts them so far from the reality that I don't even bother to try and explain it.—*Maureen Berger, BC*

Once, early on, I got lots of assumptions that if we homeschooled we must be Christian and "pro-life." Later, the assumption turned to "must be Republican," which always amused me. School reform was always such a liberal undertaking that to have it come to be connected with conservatism was kind of a hoot.

On the other hand, people have acted surprised that our kids watched *Power Rangers* or *Ninja Turtles*. Others have been surprised that we weren't vegetarian.

I sent another homeschooler a gift once, and turned a corndog box inside out to ship it in. She seemed truly disturbed at the idea that we would honestly own and consume corndogs. (I didn't notice until later that the corndogs were made from *organic* chicken.)—*Sandra Dodd, NM*

The most common assumption has been that we homeschool for religious reasons. From strangers, that didn't really surprise me, because those were the homeschoolers in the news in the early days of out homeschooling. But when a college friend who I thought knew both of us much better than that made the same comment, I was flabbergasted.

Other common assumptions were that we were exceptionally patient and unselfish, super-organized and efficient, politically on the far left or the far right, hippie radicals or religious conservatives, martyrs or just crazy. While I am fairly patient, I'm quite selfish; I had no desire to have to put my children back together after the schools messed them up. I'm only fair-to-middling on the organization and efficiency spectrum and a political moderate. I do like jumpers, but don't own any Birkenstocks. As for the crazy, I'll never tell.—*Carol Burris*

Q: *In your view, how has the homeschooling movement changed since you were first involved?*

Better and worse. It's better in that we don't get the third degree for being out in public during school hours. "Oh, why aren't you in school?" Every old biddy felt like she had the right to grill me about my children. Some things are worse because the school district has been portraying everyone who chooses differently as the enemy.—*Shannon Anderson, MN*

Things are much better than they were. I remember when my mom pulled me out of school, I was in the gifted program, and before they would allow her to homeschool, she had to prove to them that she could provide me with that same level of education as I was getting in the public school gifted program. We also used to be afraid to go out during school hours—it wasn't unknown for parents to be arrested because the police knew nothing about homeschooling.—*Myranda Brown, SC*

I hate to say it, but some of the changes I'm seeing are not good. When I started homeschooling in 1990, the established legal standing of homeschooling here in Texas was a relatively new thing. I personally knew a family that had only a few years earlier been run out of town—they'd packed everything up and disappeared over a weekend—when the school district started threatening to jail the parents for homeschooling. Because we had such an immediate understanding of the fight that had gone on to legalize homeschooling, we appreciated what homeschooling was and the fact that we could very easily have not won the right to homeschool openly. We understood that, for all that we had won in the courts, the battles were going to continue and we would have to carefully guard what had been so hard won. We also got the fact that what we were doing in educating our children was our responsibility.

But now, sixteen years later, a disturbing number of the newer homeschoolers are different. Where we took our time to research, many now want everything handed to them on a silver platter. Too often I hear something along the lines of "Look, just tell me what program to buy." This is such a huge mistake; it completely misses the point that every family, and every child in every family, comes with unique gifts and needs. It opens a family up to swallowing the wrong curriculum and deciding that homeschooling doesn't work, when, in fact, it could have worked very well if they'd only entered into it the right way.

Having said all that, though, I must say that this isn't even remotely an accurate picture of all homeschoolers—it's just something I've seen more and more in recent years. For the most part, homeschoolers are a fantastic bunch of open-minded, interactive, fascinated-by-life people who are a joy to be around and a tremendous blessing to their families.—*Tammy Cardwell, TX*

People used to be more afraid than they are now—less confident. Outsiders used to express disgust or disbelief more easily than they do now. Now it seems everyone knows an unschooling family they respect, so explanations can be shorter and less defensive.—*Sandra Dodd, NM*

It used to be you could say you were homeschooled and you could leave it at that. People wouldn't ask that many questions. They might say, "Oh, gee, that sounds cool," and leave it at that. Now they want more specifics.—*Donald Burris, FL*

Frankly, I don't like a lot of what I see, although I'm aware that there's good that comes with the bad. The school-at-home mentality is a lot more rampant now—and I see lots of parents of very young children advising other parents on how to do it, while brushing aside input from more relaxed and experienced parents of homeschool grads. Newcomers to homeschooling are often told that the first thing they need to do is "pick a style or method." Makes me wince. It causes undue concern, confusion, and misunderstanding. "I'm still trying to decide what style I'm going to be," some say, instead of just paying attention to the specific and unique needs of their own children. Way too much focus on parents and schools and curricula—way too little attention to letting children learn in their own best ways.

Among those who are interested in unschooling, I hear reports of people being discouraged from trying that path because of collisions with rigid attitudes at park days and online about what unschooling is and how it's supposed to be done. There's entirely too much division in the homeschooling world today—it's all so unnecessary, and it's the children who lose out most because of it. —*Lillian Jones, CA*

More new homeschooling parents seem to be looking for someone to give them a how-to manual. "Just tell me what to do and I'll do it." Those of us who began homeschooling in the '80s did not have the resources currently available—books, Internet, support groups, etc. I think something is lost when the process of finding your own way, what works best for your family, is given away. A whole new set of experts take the place of the school experts. Part of what is lost is self-empowerment and with it, the strength and courage to keep going when the honeymoon period is over and life's challenges emerge.—*Carol Burris, FL*

Q: How do you feel about the movement to defend and define homeschooling, as in such projects as the "We Stand for Homeschooling" petition? Are charter schools and other public school homeschooling programs a threat to homeschooling?

Anything that gets homeschooling in a positive light into the public eye is a good thing. I don't think that charter schools and other similar programs are a threat to homeschooling per se, but people do need to be careful and read those bills! Many states try to slip extra homeschooling guidelines into those same pieces of legislation, and it's up to us to identify them and demand that they be removed. Homeschooling isn't for everyone, and that's a fact. The more options there are, the better all around for everyone, especially the children.—*Myranda Brown, SC*

I don't really like how charter school and homeschooling have become synonymous. I personally would like to be left alone to homeschool as I see fit. I like the autonomy that using the private school affidavit in California affords us. I like not answering to anyone. I don't want homeschooling defined because *any* definition would be too narrow to encompass us all. Why do we even need to define it on a state or national level? I think our definition within our home changes so much that trying to define it even on our family level would be near impossible.—*Leslie Buchanan, CA*

The laws are so different state to state that I think claims of "threat to homeschooling" must needs be false. If something is a threat to one state or province's existing laws, then it should be handled at that level. There are states in which no threat whatsoever exists. Those who take a national or international stance that the sky is falling do so to take advantage of people and their fears in one way or another. It invariably has to do with politics and money. —*Sandra Dodd, NM*

My name is on the "We Stand for Homeschooling" petition, and I'm very concerned about the impact that charter schools and other pubic school-sponsored programs, billing themselves as homeschool programs, will have on legitimate homeschooling. Mind you, they may well be good programs that can serve great purposes. My concern is that they are being billed as homeschool programs and homeschoolers are accepting that label far too readily. I'm a skeptic where the government is concerned and I am convinced that if programs such as these are accepted by the masses as homeschool programs, then, eventually, the government will use the fact that "homeschoolers have already accepted our control in this area" to excuse taking more control of homeschooling. I will take staying free to homeschool over getting a free computer any day of the week.—*Tammy Caldwell, TX*

Q: How do you feel about the increasing availability of commercially produced homeschooling materials, either specific books and materials or complete programs, such as K12?

I don't think they're good for homeschooling families at all. They foster the belief that learning takes place in a linear fashion, following a set pace and order, keeping families tied to schoolbooks, tests, homework, and worksheets. In other words, they keep people thinking that they need to make their home into a mini-school. This is just not true. Real learning flourishes in the absence of arbitrary curriculum. Real learning involves observation, questions, and connections that happen in the mind of the learner.—*Mary Gold, OR*

I get emails every day from parents wanting to know where to buy the thing they have to buy so they can homeschool. It just blows their minds when I tell them there is *nothing* that they *have* to buy.—*Myranda Brown, SC*

These kinds of things probably delay the natural process of discovering that homeschooling isn't really so daunting and that children's learning absolutely doesn't need to be orchestrated and controlled in those predetermined increments. Over the years, I've heard people say, "Well, we tried homeschooling, but it just didn't work for us"—and on further questioning, it turns out that they had tried it only with one of those programs and their kids hated it and wouldn't "cooperate."—*Lillian Jones, CA*

Some people need a framework, and at least now they have a choice. It also might make it easier to comply with state regulations.—*Donald Burris, FL*

Homeschooling has become, to me, a lifestyle, not just a manner of ticking off the required boxes. But in an area with a lousy public education system, I would not want to prevent a family from giving it a try because of fear or intimidation, which these materials may help overcome. This is increasingly evident to me, living in post-Katrina south Louisiana where frantic decisions have had to be made and the school systems are even less able to be what they should (or even need to) be, although many are trying.

I do wish, though, that samples of programs were more widely available for trial use before families spend lots and lots of money on things that aren't really necessary or just don't work well with their children.—*Jo Craddock, LA*

Viral Learning

Q: Where do you see the homeschooling movement going in the next few decades?

Right now it seems that the entire society is on a cusp. It seems that either we'll get back to valuing self-sufficiency or we'll keep marching down into tyranny. Every little choice that we make supports one way or the other. Every time we shop at Wal-Mart or the farmers' market—every time we send a credit card bill in or save.

Do we trust parents to parent children—or do we need a team of social workers to watch over every household? Do we encourage children to think or should they just ride welfare?—*Shannon Anderson, MN*

People take a lot for granted today. I think they would be wise to become better acquainted with the history of homeschooling. My son made an interesting remark recently when he was fresh out of a semester of studying revolution in depth in college. I mentioned to him that I hear more and more about people flocking to the programs. He responded, "Oh, yeah! After any sort of radical revolutionary movement, there has always been a knee-jerk reaction toward conservatism through which new ideas are co-opted into something that can be profitable for a traditional power structure. Every single revolution has always followed that pattern."—*Lillian Jones, CA*

If anyone is attached to a "homeschooling movement" instead of being attached to the idea of helping her own children in their lives, I think there's some misplaced attachment, personally.—*Sandra Dodd, NM*

We will always need people who are vigilant and committed to protecting educational freedom. We ill always need the books and magazines and online information. I am afraid we will need to protect our freedom in states like mine where we have been left alone for so long. But I think when an issue arises, people will organize together to deal with it.—*Leslie McColgin, KY*

I homeschool because I think it is the best alternative for my children. I don't subscribe to a movement and I don't try to persuade others to homeschool. I'm satisfied with the freedoms I have to homeschool and have no desire to make waves about changing legislation or changing schools' accommodations for homeschoolers. If education itself becomes so diversified that the term "homeschooling" becomes a quaint anachronism, that would be fine with me. I'm not concerned with the momentum or loss of momentum of a movement.—*Christine Sanders, IA*

Q: What about activism in fields other than homeschooling (politics in general, environmentalism, sports, the arts, any kind of volunteerism)? Has it been part and parcel of the process or more of an escape or break from homeschooling?

We have at various times been helping in causes such as raising money for homeless shelters, volunteering at the humane society, or supporting a particular political cause. It's not something we did in an organized fashion. We simply followed our passions and acted when moved to do so. Since we are an unschooling family, we don't take a break from homeschooling. Unschooling is our lifestyle and our day-to-day practice—we're always learning. So any of these activities included the kids and became a part of their education.—*Mary Gold, OR*

Every time I've become involved in these things, I've found that I end up needing to pull back some. There's so much that needs to be done, and you could easily devote your whole life to any one of the issues. So I contribute a little here and a little there, but I just don't have the emotional energy at this time to plunge right in. I'm looking right now for something I can do locally to make a contribution without getting in over my head.—*Lillian Jones, CA*

Strangely, I've let all the politics slide for the lifetimes of these two girls, yet they are far more like me in their passion to change the world than my first two kids, during whose early years I was actively involved. I suppose I have been spending more time conveying my world view to them.—*Maureen Berger, BC*

Volunteering has been a part of my life since before I was a teenager. I don't see it as directly related to homeschooling at all except that both are part of the lifestyle I choose to follow. Similarly, I consider myself a conservationist (rather than an environmentalist) but that, too, is expressed in charitable donations and the choices I make every day in living my life.

If this is activism, then I do it in very quiet ways.—*Carol Burris, FL*

Q: *What do you consider the three most important things for new homeschoolers to know as they're starting out?*

You—the parents—are homeschoolers too. You are not homeschooling facilitators: you may be driving the bus but you go anywhere your passengers do.—*Julia Biales, NY*

• Look at what your children *want* before you start whipping the credit card around. Chances are you can do just as well with the things already in your house as the "latest and best" new curricula.

• Your child isn't a label. Not a diagnosis and not a grade. You can learn tons about the second grade reading process—but that isn't going to change how little Billy learns best. Value their personal process more than the "expert says."

• Scholastics can wait. It's great that the neighbor kid can read at two, but you'll never hear about his problems with math or how much bribery he needs to clean his room. It's not a race, it's all a long process. Self-care, life skills, and socializing are just as important as the War of 1812—okay, probably more important than memorizing the details of the War of 1812.—*Shannon Anderson, MN*

• You don't need a school structure for children to learn. It's okay and even preferable to follow your child's interests and pace.

• Get online and inform yourself about the different types of homeschooling options. Know what's out there. Join an e-list and a local support group. Get connected with other homeschooling families.

• Enjoy your family! You can do this.—*Mary Gold, OR*

• It's got to be enjoyable for everyone, not all the time, but at least a majority of the time. If it's too frustrating for any one, it's not going to be worth it.

• Step out of the school box, and use your imagination. You don't have to follow anyone else's plan for your life or for your child's life.

• Be confident. Family and friends, spouse and children, will all feel better about your decision if you are confident in your decision. —*Myranda Brown, SC*

• Your family is unique with unique needs. Do not cop out; research and find what is right for you.

• It's not illegal to drop a curriculum that isn't working. Yes, it may have been an expensive purchase, but it's more expensive to let a badly-fitting curriculum damage your child's will to learn.

• It is not your job to make sure your child has no learning gaps. (Learning gaps are unavoidable. There is too much knowledge in the world.) It is your job to make sure he loves learning and has the tools he needs to learn.—*Tammy Caldwell, TX*

• Get straight on the legalities in your area. The best way to do this is through state and local homeschooling support groups, and these can generally be found online. Look into support groups as well—they're invaluable, even if they might seem like a bit of bother at first.

• Homeschooling is going to be a lot different than you think —different from most things you've experienced. The sooner you can leave all your old school ideas behind, the sooner you and your children can get on with real growth and learning. In the beginning, if your children have been in school, it's pretty much a universal necessity to allow for a nice long decompression period that gives them a chance to relax and grow back into themselves, becoming natural learners again little by little. It's not time lost but time well invested. That time also gives you a chance to begin to deschool yourself and be ready to join them in a whole new kind of adventure.

• You absolutely do not need to "pick a style" or "pick a method" or "pick a curriculum"—you will greatly benefit from starting by just hanging out with and enjoying your children while you get to know one another all over again without the artificial stresses and expectations school may have caused. Everything will fall into place in good time. Relax and enjoy above all.—*Lillian Jones, WA*

- They may have many more options than they may be aware of.
- Kids *want* to learn and they *will* learn without being coerced, baited, tricked or forced.
- Playing *is* learning and that you can learn and teach so much just playing with your wonderful, exciting, smart kids.—*Leslie Buchanan, CA*

- You will be amazed at how quickly the time goes—cherish every moment and never wish away the stage the kids are at.
- Kids are very able to look out for their own interests much earlier than most people believe, providing they are knowledgeable. Give them information but don't take over their job of educating, protecting, or caring for themselves.
- Get support from others, but trust your instincts.—*Maureen Berger, BC*

- Live in the moment.
- Know that you have choices; make peaceful and joyful choices.
- Be your child's partner, not his adversary. (I learned that in La Leche League, and it has served as a good basis for my relationships with my children ever since.)—*Sandra Dodd, NM*

- Enjoy your lives together.
- Don't worry about gaps in learning; everyone has them.
- Meaningful conversation is one of the best learning tools that exists—it has worked for humanity for thousands of years!—*Leslie McColgin, KY*

- First I would say, "Congratulations! You have made a fantastic choice."
- "What materials do I need?"

"Books. The library or your personal collection. The most important thing is a 'can do' spirit."

• When you doubt your decision to homeschool, just think what the alternative is. Realize that you are not going to do a perfect job, but your worst day of homeschooling is better than their best day at institutional school."—*Donald Burris, FL*

• Familiarize yourself firsthand with the laws regarding homeschooling in your locality. Don't rely solely on others' interpretations of the law.

• Focus on growing a strong, respectful, and peaceful relationship with your children and let the academics follow.

• Work hard to really understand who your child is, validate their interests, experience their passions with them, and open your eyes to how they learn through their play and pursuit of their interests.—*Christine Sanders, IA*

• Know that unschoolers aren't doing whatever a parent thinks a child must do to learn and their kids are learning just fine.

• There is no such thing as "have to." Everything we do is a choice.

• Trying to recreate school at home is the most common cause of homeschooling failure. It's like trying to recreate the factory to make a loaf of bread at home.

(Okay, I need four.)

• School changes kids and changes the relationship they have with their parents. Parents who say "I could never spend all day with my kids" are right, in a way. They couldn't spend all day with their *schooled* kids. But living with them using the principles of unschooling and mindful parenting will allow their kids and their relationship to be what it was meant to be before school interfered. —*Joyce Fetteroll, MA*

• A bad day of homeschooling is better than the best day at school.

• You are the most important expert when it comes to your children. Listen to your heart and you will know what needs to be done.

• Just when you think you have it figured out, life changes. This is not a bad thing! You will learn and grow as much or more than your kids. Celebrate the opportunity.—*Carol Burris, FL*

• It's okay to quit a bad book. If it doesn't work, stop doing it, whether it's school, school-at-home, or even homeschooling.

• This is real: pay attention, to yourself, your partner, your children. It will all be different tomorrow, so choose to enjoy today.

• Asking for help or opinions or suggestions is not a sign of weakness, frustration or failure—the failure would be to not get help when it's needed. But discern carefully what applies to you and your situation and remember that declining help, opinions, or suggestions is a valid choice, too.—*Jo Craddock, LA*

Q: *What do you want to say that I haven't asked?*

Homeschooling isn't always what you thought it would be. Family isn't always what you thought it would be. Way back when this family began there were four of us—one male couple and one female. When Nicholas was three the other woman in the group, my partner, left. She would have said that it was the pressures of raising a disabled child, not the hope she had. The reality was even uglier—she had had two children who were taken from her in a custody battle, gay issues. Even if Nicholas hadn't been autistic, she wasn't up to what she thought she wanted. So Dan and Robert and I have gone on as a family. We lost a spouse to divorce—we had a baby die of prematurity, we have dealt with all sorts of life ups and life downs. Homeschooling remained constant—our family was as constant as we could make it for our own well-being, and because if my own parent's divorce hadn't told me so, Janet leaving certainly did: if there has to be separation, let it not be hostile.

Homeschooling is part of the art of not separating. If there are conflicts, it's easier to deal with them than try to win moral battles. Families can be anchors for society. I had to make preparations for Daniel and Robert to take over the family if I were to become too ill (or die outright) before Nicholas grew up. I'm glad they are part of my life.

It's not what four actors in college had in mind when we decided to co-parent, but it's been an interesting ride. I'm glad I lived it and look forward to what the future will bring.

I hope to see my grandchildren tread the boards, learn to read at cruising altitude, and in general, support my children as they become parents as my mentors have supported me.—*Julia Biales, NY*

Having said over and over that I don't like charter schools I would like to say that my kids are currently enrolled in one! We found a school that truly stays out of our hair, we know they want us to turn in paperwork, it is minimal and (here's the catch) we are *willing* to do the little they ask for the expanded opportunities that their funding allows us. I wish everyone in charter schools could know all their options, could know that the charter has no real jurisdiction over them, that they, the family have all the power and say-so over their kids education and they don't have to surrender their freedom to *any* school. They need to seek out charters whose philosophies fall in line with their own. I say all this because my first year homeschooling we were in a *very* strict charter—I did not know my options, I did not know *any* local homeschoolers. The Internet was beyond my reach and in its infancy. I simply didn't know that I didn't have to reduce my son to tears in an effort to teach him what the school said I had to. When I did find a support group, I found them to be too political. I did not fit in with their views and therefore no one told me that I could file a private school affidavit or that there were more charter schools in the area. I really feel it is important to be tolerant of other homeschoolers even if they are doing it exactly opposite of the way I choose to. They may have insight I don't, or they might benefit from my insight. But only if it is offered in friendship and not hostility. I am certain that there are homeschooling families who want to school at home, who want the charter school to set up a lesson plan and issue books. I know a family like this—they are happy to learn this way. The important thing is, it works for them. That is why we are homeschooling after all, isn't it? Because we get to choose what works for us.—*Leslie Buchanan, CA*

My educational philosophy:

1. Education is a lifelong process that is intimately connected to living a good and meaningful life. A good education follows naturally from living a good and meaningful life. Schooling and education are separate constructs and are not always compatible with each other. As Mark Twain said, "I never let my schooling get in the way of my education."

2. Children have a right to spend their days engaged in activities they find personally meaningful and that accomplish purposes that are clear to them in fulfilling individual, family, and community life. Real life is happening right now for every child.

3. Children have a right to decline activities that hold no personal meaning for them, that are offered for the sole purpose of teaching them something that another person has decided they ought to know.

4. Children have a right to the privacy of their minds and should be able to choose when, where, with whom, and how to communicate what they know about the world.

Because I work with children who have learning problems, I do want to say that sometimes I think there are people in the homeschool community who denigrate getting special help. I have read articles that even seem to deny the existence of significant language or learning problems. Learning problems and neurological differences and disorders do exist and there is no shame in getting professional help if a child needs physical, occupational, or speech-language therapy. In fact, with the toxic environment we live in, it's amazing children are doing as well as they are. Autism is skyrocketing to 1 in 150 children, and over the years every place I have worked has seen more and more children with clear-cut neurological problems that interfere significantly with functioning in the world. While it is true that some differences are insignificant and will not cause problems over time, there are cases of serious problems and a good therapist who is accepting of homeschooling can be of great benefit. A two-year-old not talking may just need more time, and it may be personality style or something insignificant, but that same child might have a very severe apraxia or autism and early intervention can make worlds of difference. A seven-year-old not reading may simply need more time or they might need visual exercises or phonological awareness and/or language therapy. It isn't always easy to tell and mistakes in diagnosis are made, but I don't think people should feel guilty if they pursue therapy. I don't think "experts" should be blindly trusted, but they shouldn't be completely disregarded either.

I don't think we see the stories in the homeschool literature where the kid couldn't read at 7, still not at 12, and still not at 16, and I know they exist. Just like I don't think we hear about social adjustment difficulties in late teens or early 20's. I recall a woman who co-authored a book on homeschooling on a shoestring or something like that, and I can't recall her name. But she stayed at our home with her daughter for a day or two, having gotten our name out of the *Growing Without Schooling* directory. At that time she had a son in his late 20's who she had homeschooled after adopting him, removing him from a negative school situation around middle childhood. She said she regretted not doing more to directly help him with his learning difficulties, and he was struggling a lot as an adult.

Therapy doesn't have to be didactic and there are people like me who work collaboratively with families to support their goals and who believe in child-led learning. I suggest people look for therapy and help outside of the public school setting. There are many other options.—*Leslie McColgin, KY*

I have one big wish—that more people coming into homeschooling today could understand the vision so many of us have come to see and love and realize. There's so much more that can be accomplished than just turning out learning robots. Homeschooling isn't just about working through a curriculum, memorizing facts, and honing skills—even if it includes doing those workbooks on "critical thinking." Homeschooling can produce creative individuals who think outside the box and have the capacity to do whatever they set their minds on—but that can't happen so easily through some of the stifling processes that abound today. If you're going to step outside the campus model, why not go a bit farther and try something really different? People don't need experts and programs to tell them how to do it—there is no "it," anyway, and that's actually a good thing. Life is a lot bigger and offers a lot more possibilities and opportunities outside the "it" mentality.—*Lillian Jones, WA*

Further Reading

As I mentioned earlier in this book, I read a lot of books.
When I first began to think about homeschooling, I read a lot
of books about homeschooling, and when I began to write my
own books, I read even more books about homeschooling,
about learning and cognitive psychology, about the history of
education, and the sociology of families and childhood.

As my daughters reached their late teens and beyond, I've
found myself reading more about technology and its effects
on society in general and on families and schools in particular,
which has undoubtedly influenced my thinking, to the point
that my favorite homeschooling books are no longer explicitly
about homeschooling. This list includes books which
provoked and stimulated me, most favorably, but a few
somewhat less positively. All of them were interesting reading.

(I've always intended a personal rather than academic style
for this book, and deliberately chose not to include endnotes.

Further Reading

If you're interested in where I came up with particular facts or ideas, please feel free to email me at marygriff@mac.com.)

Bissex, Glenda L. (1980).*Gnys at Wrk: A Child Learns to Write and Read.* Cambridge, MA: Harvard University Press.

Coles, Gerald (1998). *Reading Lessons: The Debate Over Literacy.* New York: Hill and Wang.

Coontz, Stephanie (1992). *The Way We Never Were: American Families and the Nostalgia Trap.* New York: Basic Books.

Coontz, Stephanie (1997). *The Way We Really Are: Coming to Terms with America's Changing Families.* New York: Basic Books.

Deci, Edward L., with Richard Flaste (1995). *Why We Do What We Do: Understanding Self-Motivation.* New York: Penguin Books.

Education Week (2000). *Lessons of a Century: A Nation's Schools Come of Age.* Bethesda, MD: Editorial Projects in Education.

Ehrenreich, Barbara, and Deirdre English (1978). *For Her Own Good: 150 Years of the Experts' Advice to Women.* New York: Anchor Books.

Ericsson, K. Anders, ed., et al. (2006). *Cambridge Handbook of Expertise and Expert Performance.* Cambridge, UK: Cambridge University Press.

Gould, Stephen J. (1981). *The Mismeasure of Man.* New York: W. W. Norton.

Greven, Philip ((1990). *Spare the Child: The Religious Roots of Punishment and the Psychological Impact of Physical Abuse.* New York: Alfred A. Knopf.

Griffith, Mary (1999). *The Homeschooling Handbook: From Preschool to High School, a Parent's Guide* (Second Ed.). New York: Three Rivers Press.

Griffith, Mary (1998). *The Unschooling Handbook: How to Use the Whole World As Your Child's Classroom.* New York: Three Rivers Press.

Hayes, Charles D. (1998). *Beyond the American Dream: Lifelong Learning and the Search for Meaning in a Postmodern World.* Wasilla, AK: Autodidactic Press.

Heins, Marjorie (2001). *Not in Front of the Children: "Indecency," Censorship, and the Innocence of Youth.* New York: Hill and Wang.

Hersch, Patricia (1998). *A Tribe Apart: A Journey into the Heart of American Adolescence.* New York: Fawcett Columbine.

Hine, Thomas (1999). *The Rise & Fall of the American Teenager.* New York: Bard/Avon.

Hodgson, Lucia (1997). *Raised in Captivity: Why Does America Fail Its Children?* St. Paul, MN: Graywolf Press.

Hulbert, Ann (2003). *Raising America: Experts, Parents, and a Century of Advice About Children.* New York: Alfred A. Knopf.

Johnson, Steven (1997). *Interface Culture: How New Technology Transforms the Way We Create & Communicate.* New York: Basic Books.

Johnson, Steven (2001). *Emergence: The Connected Lives of Ants, Brains, Cities, and Software.* New York: Scribner.

Johnson, Steven (2005). *Everything Bad Is Good For You: How Today's Popular Culture Is Actually Making America Smarter.* New York: Riverhead Books.

Kismaric, Carole, and Marvin Heiferman (1996). *Growing Up with Dick and Jane: Learning and Living the American Dream.* San Francisco: Collins Publishers.

Kohn, Alfie (1986). *No Contest: The Case Against Competition.* New York: Houghton Mifflin.

Kohn, Alfie (1993). *Punished by Rewards: The Trouble with Gold Stars, Incentive Plans, A's, Praise, and Other Bribes.* New York: Houghton Mifflin.

Kozol, Jonathan (1991). *Savage Inequalities: Children in America's Schools.* New York: Crown.

Lemann, Nicholas (1999). *The Big Test: The Secret History of the*

American Meritocracy. New York: Farrar Straus and Giroux.

Louv, Richard (1990). *Childhood's Future*. New York: Houghton Mifflin.

Males, Mike A. (1996). *The Scapegoat Generation: America's War on Adolescents*. Monroe, ME: Common Courage Press.

Males, Mike A. (1999). *Framing Youth: 10 Myths about the Next Generation*. Monroe, ME: Common Courage Press.

Manguel, Alberto ((1996). *A History of Reading*. New York: Viking Penguin.

Molnar, Alex (1996). *Giving Kids the Business: The Commercialization of America's Schools*. Boulder, CO: Westview Press.

Nasaw, David (1979). *Schooled to Order: A Social History of Public Schooling in the United States*. New York: Oxford University Press.

Ohanian, Susan (1999). *One Size Fits Few: The Folly of Educational Standards*. Portsmouth, NH: Heineman.

Owen, David, with Marilyn Doerr (1999). *None of the Above: The Truth Behind the SATs* (Rev. Ed.). Lanham, MD: Rowman & Littlefield.

Palladino, Grace (1996). *Teenagers: An American History*. New York: Basic Books.

Perelman, Lewis J. (1992). *School's Out: Hyperlearning, the New Technology, and the End of Education*. New York: Morrow.

Robbins, Alexandra (2006). *Overachievers: The Secret Lives of Driven Kids*. New York: Hyperion.

Sacks, Peter (1999). *Standardized Minds: The High Price of America's Testing Culture and What We Can Do to Change It*. Cambridge, MA: Perseus Books.

Schwartz, Lynee Sharon (1996). *Ruined by Reading: A Life in Books*. Boston: Beacon Press.

Silberman, Arlene (1989). *Growing Up Writing: Teaching Our Children to Write, Think, Learn*. Portsmouth, NH: Heineman.

Smith, Frank (1985). *Reading Without Nonsense* (2nd Ed.). New York: Teachers College Press.

Smith, Frank (1986). *Insult to Intelligence: the Bureaucratic Invasion of Our Classrooms.* Portsmouth, NH: Heineman.

Smith, Frank (1988). *Joining the Literacy Club: Further Essays into Education.* Portsmouth, NH: Heineman.

Smith, Frank (1998). *The Book of Learning and Forgetting.* New York: Teachers College Press

Smith, Frank (2002). *The Glass Wall: Why Mathematics Can Seem Difficult.* New York: Teachers College Press.

Stearns, Peter N. (2003). *Anxious Parents: A History of Modern Childrearing in America.* New York: New York University Press.

Straus, Murray A. (1994). *Beating the Devil Out of Them: Corporal Punishment in American Families.* New York: Lexington Books.

Sulloway, Frank J. (1996). *Born to Rebel: Birth Order, Family Dynamics and Creative Lives.* New York: Pantheon.

Tapscott, Donald, and Anthony D. Williams (2006). *Wikinomics: How Mass Collaboration Changes Everything.* New York: Portfolio/Penguin.

Printed in the United States
124878LV00006B/155/A

LP516   110   9 781430 312178